This Son of Mine. . .

Discovering Your True Identity in the Love of God

Malcolm Smith

This Son of Mine. . .
Discovering Your True Identity in the Love of God
by Malcolm Smith

Printed in the United States of America

Edited by Xulon Press

ISBN 9781498433945

www.xulonpress.com

I invite you to join me on a journey into the amazing story that Jesus told of the father and his two sons. The general outline of the story is well known, but seeing its movements through the eyes of the first hearers, listening through the customs of that people, and hearing it as they heard it opens up new horizons that can be missed if we read it through our Western eyes. It becomes quickly obvious that this is not a soft sentimental mushy story of a loser coming home. Jesus is revealing the God-who-is-love in stark contrast to the false god of accusation and judgment who is exposed and dismantled in this story. The parable constitutes the war cry of the Prince of Peace! Jesus is throwing down the gauntlet to the religious leaders and their teaching that held the populace in fear and bondage. It is a story that will set every human free.

Take the hand of the Holy Spirit and come with me into the most radical story that Jesus every told.

Acknowledgments

When I was about fifteen years old, I read a sermon by C. H. Spurgeon on the prodigal son, and I was hooked! I have spent the last sixty years reading any material I could lay my hands on that would give further insight to this story. I am sorry that I did not keep a list of those books and articles, but to every author and preacher who has aided my meditations—thank you.

One person must be mentioned, a man who passed through my life in my mid teenage years. I knew him simply as Sam. He had lived in the Bible lands for most of his life, much of the time as a missionary. He returned to England once a year, and as we visited, I listened to his description of life in the villages of the Bible, almost unchanged in thousands of years. He brought with him the clothes and household items of the peasants of the Galilee and Judea, and I dressed in the clothes of the shepherds and fisher folk of the Galilee; I put the robes of the upper class around my shoulders while handling the simple kitchenware of the people. As I listened to his stories of life in the villages and dressed in these clothes, I was transported back in time to the world of the Bible. Later my own studies in the covenant gave me the worldview of the people who populated the pages of the Scriptures. Sam is now with the Lord, but his insights have enriched all my understanding of Scripture.

Thanks to my wife Nancy with whom I sit for hours on our porch and explore together the wonders of God's love. These pages contain revelations that we have had together in those conversations. She has hounded me for years to write this book, and there is no question that it would never have been but for her persistence.

Thank you, Holy Spirit, constant friend, teacher, revealer of the Son, guide into the heart of the Father, giver of wisdom and understanding not only of the beauty of the Father and Son but also of our glory in union with Christ Jesus the Lord.

Contents

1

Revelation of Agape

This is a story about love, but in the culture of twenty-first century love can mean many things—especially in a story like this one. We will not know what is happening here until we are clear about this word *love*. This is not a sentimental story meant to bring tears to the eyes and a lump in our throat as we tie yellow ribbons on the front gate. It is not the feeling about someone who gives us personal pleasure. It is not sheep-eyed romantic love, nor is it the feeling about someone that is translated into immediate sex. This love does not draw circles and love all those who think, look, or believe as I do. It is not even the high and noble love of a human in giving his or her life for another. The fact is that human love at its highest and best has within it a fatal flaw. This is a story intended to reveal and open us to the possibilities of God-love. God-love was always present in the spiritual darkness of mankind as a thin shaft of light until it blazed forth fully revealed in the person of Jesus Christ.

The God-love in Christ is the greatest personal force in and beyond the universe, bringing rebirth and resurrection to mankind, restoring and recreating the human to the original purpose for which we were created.

What is this love? The word in the Greek language of the New Testament is "*agape.*" *Agape* describes God's limitless personal relentless energy moving to fulfill His original purpose in creating mankind that we should be in His image and likeness. *Agape* describes ultimate relationship within God that will not rest until He brings us to participate in that relationship.

God is *agape*. *Agape* is not an occasional trait, a mood he may or may not presently have. *Agape* is not something that God has, a possession to increase or decrease or be used up; *agape* is who God *is* and whatever is true of God, whatever He does, all is the expression of this God-love.

Agape is not the response to one whose beauty excites and overtakes him, but arising from who He *is*; it springs spontaneously from His heart. His love originates in who He is, not in the beauty of the beloved. God does not fall in love—He is love! For this reason *agape* is unconditional love invading the darkness and ugliness of man's sin to embrace and go to death to bring even the enemy into His saving embrace.

Agape is infinitely for us, standing with us against all the powers that would seek to separate us from Him. *Agape* does not label us but delights in every human as we are and what we shall be.

Agape is like light breaking up into many colors, like a diamond with many facets. It is revealed as forgiveness, releasing us from the guilt and power of sin; it is limitless goodness, compassion, kindness, tenderness, gentleness, patience, and faithfulness to name but a few.

The central truth that God is *agape* is the key to understanding the full revelation of God that Jesus gave to us. He revealed that God is not a solitary one, but the one of union, of the relationship of three in the perfect union of love. Love does not exist in solitary self-contemplation but in joyous movement toward the other. God is not a noun but a verb! Within God is the limitless action of love giving, love receiving, love delighting in, and celebrating the other.

The God of the Old Testament, Yahweh, was revealed by Jesus to be the three, the Father, the Son, and the Holy Spirit, one in purpose, will, mind, and action—interdependent and bound together in limitless love. Not three gods but each dependent upon and living freely in and receiving life from the other, delighting in the other, each giving place to the other in perfect harmony, joy, and trust. This perfect dwelling in love is the God-life Jesus called eternal life.

Agape is the personal relentless and unwavering move to union—life found and celebrated in the other's embrace; it wills no separation, masking, or hiding and moves to overcome all that would divide or separate. It is the unbegun source of life, joy, peace, and unlimited possibilities.

Agape is the answer to the question that asks the meaning of life. God-love willed to bring into being a creature that bore His image and likeness, to share and participate in the life-that-is-love—a created being who would find home in the midst of the love that flowed between the Father, Son, and Spirit. Mankind, a creature finding life in fellowship and dependence upon the life of the Creator, the life that is *agape.* The man and the woman were created to reflect and reveal God-love in creation—created beings made to live the God-life within the time-space ordinary life of the creature.

The great tragedy was in the human listening and yielding to the lie of Satan, lured by the illusion that there were limitless possibilities of human potential beyond the possibility of God-love. Satan assured them that true life was to be found independently of the love-life of God; their declaration of independence was the door to discovering themselves to be gods dependent upon no one finding life within their own created self. The man and the woman were seduced by the promise; they took the bait and trusted the lie. But they did not enter life; instead they found themselves separated from it, entering into death—separation from the only true life and home within the fellowship of *agape* in the heart of God.

Satan is the divider, the separator. Through his lie he separated mankind from God, from each other and brought about chaos and division within the individual human person. The division was death and destruction to mankind and through Him, the entire creation. The meaning of the word "sin" is to miss the mark, to build something that is not according to the original and only design. Sin is not merely the breaking of rules; it is the willful departure from the blueprint of mankind's existence, which is relationship with God, dwelling in *agape.*

What shall God do in response to Adam's sin? He answered that question with a revelation of *agape* that was infinitely greater than the sin that challenged Him. He announced the plan of *agape* to overcome the separation and bring mankind to the original purpose of union: relationship with God. Where man's sin abounded, the relentless grace of *agape* did much more abound! He does not shut the door to His heart but unconditionally leaves it open. *Agape* takes the initiative to save the race, announcing that He will come and personally undo the lie, unravel Satan's purpose of death, and restore mankind to fellowship in *agape.*

Agape is finally defined in the ultimate self-giving of God in the gift of Jesus the Son of God. Jesus is God the Son entering the human race, *agape* seeking and saving the lost.

John 3: 16 states, "For God so loved the world that. . ." The text does not merely inform us that God loved the world but defines that love once and for all in the specific act of God, ". . . *that* He gave His only begotten Son. . ."

Any definition of God-love that does not ultimately focus in the person of Jesus Christ, His death, resurrection, and ascension is not the agape-love described in the Scripture. *The glory of God, God-love, is clearly seen and imaged in the face of Jesus.*

The only response that the human can make to agape is faith that trusts and surrenders to Him, resting all hope in the agenda of God revealed in Jesus.

Jesus is infinitely more than the prophet his first hearers thought Him to be. In Jesus, God became flesh, entered into our humanity, and joined us in the ghetto of sin and death. He claimed that He was the final and ultimate revelation of the one true God in His person, words, and actions. He healed the sick and set people free from the tormenting bondage to Satan. He came where we are to embrace us and give us His own life entering into and conquering our death to bring us home in His resurrection into the relationship and union with the Father in which He eternally lived,

He did not merely bring the words of God; He was the Word made flesh, one of us.

John 1:18 states the fact succinctly:

> No man has seen God at any time; the only begotten God, who is in the bosom of the Father, He has explained Him.

The Amplified Bible puts it even more clearly:

> No man has ever seen God at any time; the only unique Son, or the only begotten God, Who is in the bosom [in the intimate presence] of the Father, He has declared Him [He has revealed Him and brought Him out where He can be seen; He has interpreted Him and He has made Him known].

The peasants were amazed at His words and stood astonished at His works; the temple fumed with rage and wanted to be rid of Him as He exposed them as representatives not of God but of the liar. Rome, the latest expression of the god of cruel power, watched. Their spies were listening and waiting for any suggestion of insurrection in His words that would threaten their iron rule.

And when His mission seemed to begin to have unstoppable traction, He did the one thing that shocked everyone—friend and enemy alike. He ate with tax gatherers—the outcasts of all that was moral, decent, and holy.

At that time He gave us this parable. Here is Jesus giving definition to *agape*, the love of the Father who sent Him, the love that He reveals in His life and will ultimately display in His death and resurrection. He is the faithful witness of the heart of God and here gives us a report of God's feelings toward us.

The courtyard in Galilee is the war zone where the truth faces off with the liar.

2

The Revolutionary

Now all the tax-gatherers and the sinners were coming near Him to listen to Him. And both the Pharisees and the scribes began to grumble, saying, "This man receives sinners and eats with them."

The scene is a party where there is laughter and free flow of conversation; the majority of the guests were obviously upper class, above the average income of peasants of the Galilee. Scattered among them were a few who by their dress and demeanor were obviously peasants. This also showed by their discomfort; they were more at home in the markets and fishing boats on the nearby Lake Galilee than in this high-class crowd.

Everyone's attention was on the young peasant who dominated the ongoing conversation at the table—Jesus the carpenter prophet from one of the towns around the lake.

As such meals often were, this one was in an open courtyard, and curious neighbors were gathered around the perimeter straining to hear every word that the young man was saying. Among the crowd were some of the local religious leaders; some of them might even have traveled up from Jerusalem to investigate what Jesus was teaching.

These religious leaders were members of an extreme sect within Judaism called Pharisees; they dressed in long flowing robes, mostly blue in color, and wore little boxes containing verses of the Torah—the Law of Moses—on their right arm and on their forehead. Their attention was focused on Jesus; their lips curled in disgust and horror. They muttered to one another in loud whispers that could be heard by those at the table and carried to other listeners around the courtyard. They almost spat out the words in their disgust while thinly disguising their excitement that they had trapped

Him in a compromising situation; *"He eats with tax collectors and with sinners"* they hissed to one another.

The men at the table in their fine robes were tax collectors, and with them were characters with dubious reputation. Tax collectors were Jews who had betrayed their own people, forsaken their faith, and sold themselves to the Romans who presently occupied Israel. The Romans employed these men who, knowing their own people, were more adept at extracting the taxes imposed by the foreign power than a Roman; the taxes were heavy, and the collectors added a percentage for themselves to add to their generous salary from Rome.

Every Jew and the Pharisee in particular hated the tax collector; every Sabbath the names of the local tax collectors were read in the synagogue worship solemnly declaring that these despicable creatures could never be forgiven. They were spat at in the street and declared an abomination to God, unclean and worse than Gentiles. They were betrayers of their own people, and having willingly bound themselves to the Gentiles, they had trashed the most precious possession of the Jewish people: their covenant relationship with the true God. Throwing in their lot with Gentiles who did not know the covenant, they were doubly condemned—knowing the truth and walking away from it, trampling underfoot the revelation God had given to Abraham, to Moses, and to Israel. The tax collectors, although the richest men in the town and living in opulence, were lonely, living with their own self-hate and inner darkness, knowing they had betrayed and sold their true selves for the shekels that filled their bank accounts.

Jesus was eating with these despised tax collectors from all over Galilee. He made no secret of it sitting in a public place for all to see. He sat at table and ate bread with these unclean pariah dogs whom all decent people vehemently believed were rejected by God.

In our Western culture our first thought in eating is to satisfy hunger. There may be other reasons we eat, but essentially we eat together because it is meal time, and we are hungry. In the countries of the Middle East eating was (and still is) a relational event. One ate bread to declare, establish, nurture, and seal a covenant relationship. To eat with someone was called “table fellowship” and meant that the persons eating at the table now stood in covenant solidarity with each other. To break bread with someone was to be involved in their life to protect and be there for them in the day of trouble and be trusted to be true to them in their absence. It meant that you would celebrate and share their success and joy as surely as you would stand with them in their failure and shame. Eating was a declaration of enduring friendship. Our word "companion" echoes more recent days when this was true in the West; *com* is the Latin word for "with" and *pan* meaning "bread"—a companion is one that you eat bread with.

In such a culture one was careful about who sat at table with him! Eating bread with a person declared such a bond of friendship that refusal to eat with someone was a great insult, and in some cases the refusal would be understood as a declaration of war!

For Jesus to eat with tax collectors was not a social blunder done in ignorance; it was not a political gaffe of a newcomer to religious politics. The solemnity of eating with someone was one of the first things that Jesus knew as a child growing up in Nazareth. He ate with these men intentionally in a deliberate public act, sending a clear message that He knew could not be misunderstood by anyone. He was announcing that He was the friend of tax collectors and sinners. He did it publicly because eating with such persons was vital and necessary to Jesus' mission.

The watchers in that courtyard did not know nor could they fathom that mission. It was beyond human comprehension. By any standards known in that world Jesus was committing social suicide by sitting at that table eating bread with the despised and outcast. His reputation and credibility would be destroyed in the eyes of all the Galilee and beyond. His mission was dead on arrival. Everyone who saw Him or heard of what He did would be scandalized. No one could comprehend a person entering into table fellowship with these betrayers of their people. He had committed the unthinkable and unforgivable religious and social crime. In the horrified eyes of the townsfolk who had gathered to look, He was now tarnished and socially unacceptable. They gathered like persons gather to see an accident and then go to tell their friends what they saw. It would be quickly repeated with horrific tone and open-mouthed shock—*"He ate with tax collectors and sinners!"*—passed by eager mouths in the markets as the fish vendors sold the latest catch, around the fishing boats as the fishermen mended their nets, with the sheep herders in the hills, and around the night meal in the little homes throughout the lake communities and scattered across the hills; the juiciest gossip of decades would be carried by traders with their donkey and camel trains down to Jerusalem and to the Mediterranean coastal towns and beyond.

Jesus makes a public point of sitting at table fellowship with them—accepting them and reversing the accepted idea that He would be contaminated with their sin by close contact with them. By sitting at table with them Jesus was refusing to label them, accepting each one of them as they were and in so doing elevating them from their given designation as pariah dogs to persons. He was standing in solidarity with them, declaring a covenant of friendship. He sat there by choice and so accepted their shame, rejection, and the hatred directed to them as His own. By sitting with them He entered into their deepest selves past their masks to their self-hatred and shame. His look of acceptance said, *"I have looked upon your deepest inner darkness and embrace you standing as one with you."* He was the seeking love of God uniting with them and in the midst of their darkness proclaimed that they were loved, forgiven, and called to a new life in union with Him. It was love that by sitting with them plainly said that He would go to any length, pay any cost, to embrace them where they were.

At that table the great exchange took place; He took and shared their shame and abomination in the eyes of society and Torah and in exchange gave them the forgiveness and full acceptance of God that had found them and sat in covenant friendship with them. By His presence at the table Jesus who is God with us announced that their sins were forgiven.

In this very public act Jesus was choosing to be humiliated, creating a scandal that would not go away. This public scandal was a major event that would eventually lead to the ultimate rejection of Him and His message by the temple authorities silencing Him in crucifixion. His table fellowship with untouchables was in fact a preview of that blood shedding in crucifixion when He would enter the darkness of the sin and curse of the world and make it His own. At that time He would become our sin and declare it swallowed by love and in His resurrection announce mankind forgiven and home in the *agape* of the Father.

Over the previous months the Pharisees had watched Him like a hawk for one word or act they could use to discredit Him before the masses who listened to Him. Finally they had what they had waited for. The Pharisees were both delighted and repulsed by what they saw in the courtyard in Galilee. The thought of eating with a tax collector was like sitting with a pig in its filth, and the sight caused acid bile to rise in their throat. They were infuriated that one who claimed to speak the words of God would be found in table fellowship with these rats of society and doing it at a party with loud laughter, without shame before the eyes of all the Galilee. But more importantly, they had caught Him in the scandalous act, and they would use it to discredit everything He said. A prophet of God would never eat with a tax collector. They would report it far and wide to the religious leaders with holy horror and sneer, *"He is the friend of tax collectors and sinners"*—the word *"friend"* carried all the covenant ideas of a committed love that stands with another in solidarity at any cost.

The tax collectors, confused and wondering, could only receive His love and acceptance and join in the party and His obvious joy at being with them.

Jesus was the only person they had met who did not despise, threaten, or demand promises of reform from them. He was the embodiment of love, seeking them out and essentially laying down His life for them. He called them simply to trust and accept the love that incredibly reached into their world where they were condemned and hated and inhale the gift of the air of divine acceptance.

Before Jesus said a word, He threw all those present into confusion; He made their heads spin as He defied every rule by which humans order their lives. Questions tumbled through the minds of religious leaders and fisher folk alike.

Could it be that the real God stood in solidarity with the outcasts of society? And if with them, then surely He stood with every human being. Did the real God actually like humans? Was the real God involved with anyone outside of the temple liturgies?

3

Four Stories

Jesus heard the loud whispers and saw the looks of horror and disgust on the faces of the religious leaders; He knew that His action infuriated them and would inevitably lead to the ultimate confrontation. He answered everyone in hearing distance with four stories recorded in Luke 15:3–32.

First He explains why He sits at table with tax collectors with the stories of a shepherd going into the wilderness to find his lost sheep and then of a woman turning out the house to find a coin that was lost:

> "And He told them this parable, saying, "What man among you, if he has a hundred sheep and has lost one of them, does not leave the

ninety-nine in the open pasture, and go after the one which is lost, until he finds it? And when he has found it, he lays it on his shoulders, rejoicing. And when he comes home, he calls together his friends and his neighbors, saying to them, 'Rejoice with me, for I have found my sheep which was lost!' I tell you that in the same way, there will be *more* joy in heaven over one sinner who repents, than over ninety-nine righteous persons who need no repentance.

Or what woman, if she has ten silver coins and loses one coin, does not light a lamp and sweep the house and search carefully until she finds it? And when she has found it, she calls together her friends and neighbors, saying, 'Rejoice with me, for I have found the coin which I had lost!' In the same way, I tell you, there is joy in the presence of the angels of God over one sinner who repents."

And then He tells the story of the lost son and the love of a father who could not rest until his son was home in his arms:

"And He said, "A certain man had two sons; and the younger of them said to his father,' Father, give me the share of the estate that falls to me.' And he divided his wealth between them. And not many days later, the younger son gathered everything together and went on a journey into a distant country, and there he squandered his estate with loose living. Now when he had spent everything, a severe famine occurred in that country and he began to be in need. And he went and attached himself to one of the citizens of that country, and he sent him into his fields to feed swine. And he was longing to fill his stomach with the pods that the swine were eating, and no one was giving *anything* to him. But when he came to his senses, he said, 'How many of my father's hired men have more than enough bread, but I am dying here with hunger! I will get up and go to my father, and will say to him, "Father, I have sinned against heaven, and in your sight; I am no longer worthy to be called your son; make me as one of your hired men.' And he got up and came to his father.

> But while he was still a long way off, his father saw him, and felt compassion *for him,* and ran and embraced him, and kissed him. And the son said to him, 'Father, I have sinned against heaven and in your sight; I am no longer worthy to be called your son.' But the father said to his slaves, 'Quickly bring out the best robe and put it on him, and put a ring on his hand and sandals on his feet; and bring the fattened calf, kill it, and let us eat and be merry; for this son of mine was dead, and has come to life again; he was lost, and has been found.' And they began to be merry."

This was followed by a fourth and interlocking story of the rage of the elder brother in the family:

> "Now his older son was in the field, and when he came and approached the house, he heard music and dancing. And he summoned one of the servants and *began* inquiring what these things might be. And he said to him, 'Your brother has come, and your father has killed the

> fattened calf, because he has received him back safe and sound.' But he became angry, and was not willing to go in; and his father came out and *began* entreating him. But he answered and said to his father, 'Look! For so many years I have been serving you, and I have never neglected a command of yours; and *yet* you have never given me a kid, that I might be merry with my friends; but when this son of yours came, who has devoured your wealth with harlots, you killed the fattened calf for him.' And he said to him, '*My* child, you have always been with me, and all that is mine is yours. But we had to be merry and rejoice, for this brother of yours was dead and *has begun* to live, and *was* lost and has been found."

He told the stories to the tax collectors at the table, knowing that every word would be heard by all the listeners around the courtyard and especially the Pharisees.

4

Broken Relationship

A certain man had two sons. . .

He grounds the story in a family. Without it beginning in a family relationship, there is no story. The son was leaving the father and the family; he went to the far country as a son rebelling against the father, not as a rootless wanderer; he returned to the home he had fled from to be welcomed by the father he had rejected.

He belongs in a family working out the relationship that comes with that belonging.

Jesus is answering the confusion and question of His audience, both tax collector and Pharisee. He answers them by placing the table of laughing tax collectors and the enraged religious leaders in the context of the story of the human race; each one of us finds ourselves somewhere in this story.

The purpose of God in creating was not merely to bring about a universe full of meaningless atoms and a high species of animals controlled by chemistry and hormones. Before there was time or space, there was the God who is love who determined to create time, space, and matter and to manifest His love in the midst of it. Creatures made from dust to unite with *agape*, form relationships that would constitute a family in His image. He brought the human family into existence out from His love, determined to shower His love on them, to bless them in every aspect of their being. They in turn would participate in His love and share His love with one another. The family loved by the Creator would be united in loving one another.

All of our inarticulate longings and sense of emptiness is grounded in our forgetting that we came into being from the love of God and that we belong in and to Him. We are not homeless disconnected entities wandering without purpose through time and space but bear the mark of divine ownership upon us.

The story is about the younger son becoming disconnected from the place of belonging and forgetting that there was once a belonging. The point of the story is that wherever the son may be and whatever he may think of the father or of his own condition, he could not disconnect from his identity as the father's son with a place in the family. As the story unfolds, we see the unconditional and unfailing love of the father, the bond and glue of the relationship, seeing through the results of the far country to the reality that this was his son that had been lost to his love. It is the father's tenacious love that brings about the son's resurrection to the relationship and restoration to the place in the family of his belonging.

Without the underlying absolute that the wandering son belonged in the father's love, there is no story. The previous parables were similarly rooted in things that had been lost from the owner. A thing cannot be lost unless it first belonged to someone. The woman engaged in a relentless search for her coin because it was hers and of great value to her was probably of little interest to anyone else. The shepherd went into the wilderness, not to hunt for a wild animal but to search for a sheep that he designated as "*my sheep.*" His dangerous mission was driven by the fact he owned the sheep and had an investment in it.

The first truth that Jesus was revealing to His audience was that these tax collectors belonged to a God they had forgotten—but a God who never ceased loving them and was determined to resurrect them to their true place of belonging in His family.

What Jesus was saying infuriated the Pharisee; it was a scandal that rocked their world. They declared the tax gatherer as outside of God's covenant and concern and certainly not bearing the mark of His ownership.

The Pharisees, like all religions, saw mankind's problem as wrong *behavior*, but Jesus is telling us it is broken *relationships,* being disconnected with the place of belonging.

A certain man had two sons. . .

The story begins before the first words of its telling. We are plunged into a story that is already well under way before we get there.

As the story unfolds we come to know the father and his relationship to the two sons. He is a man of compassion and unconditional love toward all. We come to know him as a generous man, not tight fisted but with open hand to all, even to temporary help.

His two sons were the special focus of his love. His love was spontaneous, springing immediately from his heart. It was not called into being by the good behavior of these boys nor could their lack of response to his goodness repel it. He is a man who owns his love; it is not determined by the behavior of those to whom he would give it.

Essentially the parable is about the father. The lives of the sons are defined by their relationship to the father. It is his fierce and unrelenting love that refuses to be separated from them in his heart whatever they may do. He never forgets them but unfailingly follows them from his heart wherever they go, ready and waiting to forgive and receive them.

The father and his two sons live and work together in the ranch home. The two boys enjoy all the benefits of the sons of a wealthy land owner. But neither of them had a clue about what home and the relationships that held it together were about. Both of them are confused about their identity as the sons of their father and the relationship in which that is birthed and flourishes.

A son was understood as being the image and likeness of the father to represent and so honor him by carrying his faith and values into the village life and cause him to live on in the son's life. The son was the heir of the father's property with the responsibility of fulfilling the father's life and wealth and extending it into the future. The most coveted inheritance was the blessing of the father before his death, authorizing and enabling him to fulfill his hopes and dreams in the next generation. The greatest sorrow was when a son dishonored the parent, which is the message of the Old Testament wisdom book of Proverbs.

The younger son had no interest in fulfilling his father's life and dreams. He is restless, bored with the life on the ranch with his father and brother. Israel was the main highway between continents. The roads from Europe, Asia, and the Orient converged to the north and exited through the southern boundary to Egypt and Africa. Always there would be someone from somewhere going on their way to someplace else. The traffic included travelers seeking adventure in foreign lands, caravans with their exotic wares, and those who would buy and sell in the places they travelled through. The son looked at the travelers with their pack on their back, with a far-off look in their eye and envied their independence, the freedom to go where they pleased. As he got out of bed to his day on the farm, the travelers were meeting new people in new and exotic places.

His resentment toward his father and life at the ranch and in the village grew into a smoldering bitterness. He began to hate all that his father thought, his faith, and the values he stood for. In the darkness of the night he lay and listened to the voices from beyond the fence of the ranch and the boundaries of the village, seductive whispers that called him to the open road and places far away from his father's house and control when sitting out in the field daydreaming.

He wanted love; love that he defined as fame in the eyes of friends who flocked around him and adored him for his power and success that had no connection with his being the son of his father. He would look around the ranch with disgust. "How can I be me, grow up to be the man I want to be with my father breathing down my neck, spoiling my life!"

He looked on his father as the great spoiler of life; he did not see him as the bonding glue of love that held everything and everyone together, the guiding voice of love's wisdom. He appreciated his father only as a cash cow, but even there he believed he was entitled to everything that he had, and always was the thought that he would have a lot more when the old man died.

Although the two sons lived, ate, and worked in the presence of the father's love and care, neither of them recognized it; they did not see that their life was the gift of love but their right. Since they could remember the father's love was reaching toward them, watching over them and seeking their highest good, but they neither recognized responded to, or received it. They walked as if blind and deaf oblivious to the love in which they lived. From before the story begins, the father's love is a given whether the sons understood it, believed it, or responded to it.

Both sons operated from the base of self-absorbed entitlement in the midst of the family in which the father's reality was covenant love that gave of self.

. . . and the younger of them said to his father, "Father, give me the share of the estate that falls to me." And he divided his wealth between them.

The story begins with the radical rejection of the father's love in the son's determination to exit the family, break all ties, and set up an independent life with no reference to his origin. His revised plan for his life was independence from all that his father stood for, using the money of his inheritance that he perceived as his right and power to do and be all he was now calling life.

The younger son announces that he was uprooting his life and severing ties with the family. This may not sound altogether bad to our Western ears—in fact it would sound quite normal. The time has come for the young man to leave the nest and find his fortune and independence beyond the horizon. We applaud independence.

But the culture in which Jesus delivered this story was radically different. The hearers of Jesus' words could not imagine uprooting their lives to go among strangers in order to build a life that was independent of father and relatives. That would be seen as torture, of being thrust out into intense loneliness; it would not be seen as the beginning and blossoming of life but as descent into death. Life in its fullness was understood as taking place within the love of the immediate and extended family. The family love of the village was a covenant love that bound the people and the families together in a context of *belonging.* Love and the knowledge that one belongs is the heart of life, and without those ingredients life unravels into suffering and chaos.

The young man did not only belong in his father's love but also in the hearts of his neighbors; their joys were shared by all in the village family even as their tears were felt and shared by all. Life could not be understood outside of this interdependent love that glued them together. Within this society of respect and mutual caring one understood his or her purpose in life and celebrated their place in that purpose.

To be outside of that covenant love connection was to cease to be a true person, reduced to being an individual alone and disconnected in a vast emptiness in the process of death.

If it was necessary to leave the family and clan, it would be with great sadness, and one would ask to be sent with the father's blessing and the blessing of the clan. The traveler would journey aware of the support of all left behind and would anticipate coming home as soon as possible.

This is true today in many cultures. When I first ministered among the Zulu people, I asked a man "How are you?"—I was not prepared for his answer that took an hour as he informed me of the condition of every member of his extended family, which took in most of the village! He could not conceive of an isolated individual who could simply report on his individual life taking place in separation from all his neighbors. He could only report on his own state in the context of his relationship to the extended family.

Understand the shock waves that the first words of Jesus' story sent through those who first heard his words. He is introducing a son who *wants to get away* from his family. Why is he leaving to find another home when he already has one?

But the story continued to unravel social and family norms. Not only is the son wanting to leave but doing so with a request that was a scandal, flouting the ancient law of Israel. He asked for the reading of the will and for his inheritance to be given to him even though the father was still very much alive. The law kept the property firmly in the hands of the father until death so that he would not be reduced to poverty. The young son is saying in effect, *"I cannot wait for you to die! You are a hindrance standing in the way to real life, so let's have the reading of the will and the dividing of the ranch and its assets so I can get on with my life!"*

Amazingly the father goes along with the demand. The law of Israel stated that the elder son received two thirds of the inheritance and the younger had the remaining third. The father signed over a third of the ranch to the demands of his son, who promptly turned it into cash and immediately packed his bags and headed out of town.

5

Freedom to Leave

And not many days later, the younger son gathered everything together and went on a journey into a distant country, and there he squandered his estate with loose living.

The son's departure from his family and village was not a private matter, bringing pain to the father in the privacy of his house. This is not Chicago or London but ancient Israel, and we can never impose our Western ideas of privacy into this Eastern story. In any village in Israel privacy did not exist! What happened in the father's house was the business of the entire village; the deep hurt in the father's family had a ripple effect on every family. The children swiftly carried the latest happenings of the village to everyone even as it was happening. Also the village would be made up of the extended family of this father and his sons. What the young son was doing to the father and his brother cut to the heart of everyone in the entire village, a separation from everyone who had populated his world.

But more than the horror of the exiting son was the response of the father. He let the young man proceed to liquidate the real estate, pack his bags, and leave the family. He did not threaten or restrain him. He let him go on his way.

Such a rebellious child that shamed and tore apart a family and upset the equilibrium of life in the village should have been punished in such a way that he would forget about such foolishness. He must be stopped before he destroyed himself.

The village would be confused. The only way they could interpret the father's lack of punitive action was as weakness. They however would hold their anger until such a day as the rebellious son may return.

It was an act not quickly forgotten but would be told around dinner tables and over smoldering fires for years to come. The people lived by the wisdom of the book of Proverbs, which many times over designated a son who shamed and dishonored father and mother as a fool with destruction in his path. The village family had designated this young man a fool and would be the first to administer the beating with rods that Proverbs prescribed. If such a son should return to the village, he would not only face his father's wrath but would first be met with the villagers who would take it on themselves to administer punishment with a beating before the father would even see him. To leave the community in this fashion meant that you are not coming back.

The divine love of the Father that Jesus came to reveal does not chain persons to Himself with law—as the villagers would have expected the father to do. The father was not interested in placing his young rebel under house arrest, seeking to force him to see and respond to love while he dreamed of his father's death!

The father was totally disinterested in punishing the action of his son; he did not want anything to do with a justice that satisfied the pain inflicted on him by his son's cruel action and the public shame he had brought on him and the family. He wanted his son in his arms responding to his love. If he had pursued the kind of justice the village wanted, he still would not have his son. He wanted the ache of his heart satisfied with justice that restores and makes everything right.

Love must be a freely chosen relationship, not a controlled robotic existence. The father's love could only be satisfied by love that responded to his love, a relationship that delighted in fellowship, working together in common purpose, and daily coming to know one another.

The father's love refused to force a relationship; he let the young man go with the cash of the inheritance to finance the journey to nowhere. The young son went into what could only be imagined by that culture as a terrible loneliness, a chaotic darkness, having lost the meaning to his life. The father did not lock him up in the house or imprison him as one who had lost his mind—he let him go with the cash that gave him the freedom to pursue his nightmare.

This is the story of us all. The first act that introduces us to the God-who-is-love was in the Garden of Eden (Genesis 3) confronting the insolent couple, our first parents. They had torn the fabric of creation, of their own selves, and of society by misusing love's gift of freedom in declaring their independence from His love and His love plans.

We would expect God to wipe them out as one squashes ants that upset a picnic! Start the human experiment all over again! This time make the stupid humans robots that have joyful response to love built in! But love is not a controlled mechanical robotic response. Love is birthed in freedom, not by control or manipulation.

Living life in the freedom of love was never intended to be slavishly keeping laws in an attempt to please Him and to be accepted by Him. We were created to live in joy, in freedom responding to the love of God that holds us together both as individuals and as a society. Life is not laws but knowing at heart level the love that God has for us, permeating us and in us responding to Him, doing all that he wants freely and joyfully.

On that day of the original disaster in Eden God let us go on our journey into the darkness of death. He sadly tells our first parents of the results of their choice while assuring them of his plans to right the chaos their actions had brought upon them, their children, and the entire creation. He does not do it as a cold impersonal judge announcing a life sentence but as the Father who accepts the cost and the pain of love, going to the limit in forgiving. He personally accepts the awful cost that will be incurred in restoring his children to life when He promised them the Deliverer.

The father of Jesus' story cannot and will not mock love by trying to force love in the boy; he will take it upon himself to love the boy as he is and beget his love in him. Love begets love—the boy will only know love when his eyes are opened to the unconditional love of the father, love that will resurrect him from his self-absorption to participate in that love.

Love set mankind free to follow the seducer with his great lie that real life, the home we are looking for, is to be found as far away from God-love as possible. In Adam we were set free to journey into the madness and terrifying loneliness of living death.

We are free to flee from God-the-lover but are never left alone in all our wanderings. Though blind and intoxicated with our insane surrender to the lie, *agape* relentlessly pursues us to draw us home to the only life for which we were created inside the love of God.

The father in Jesus' story would never stop hoping, looking and waiting for his son's return and restoration to the life he never knew he had.

The boy heads for the *"far country."* This is not to be thought of as far away in geography and distance but in terms of a spiritual location, far away from all that the father and the family believed and lived by. He went to a place where he could live *far away* from the faith of the family—the God they worshipped, his covenant and salvation promises, and the values that such a faith produced.

The expression is used elsewhere to describe the Gentiles, the non-Jews, outsiders to the God-who-is-love. Within the borders of Israel Gentiles lived together in non-Jewish cities that were designated as *far-away* places. The Roman army of occupation gave plenty of pockets of *"far country"* living. Jesus was probably saying that the son headed for a city where idols were worshipped and a life without reference to God could be pursued.

He arrives in such a place in a mental and emotional state he has never known before and no file to put it in. He has no family love or support or the love of friends—he is alone. But he solves that problem quickly. He has a pocket full of cash that translated into the power to change the situation. He can quickly buy a false love and empty friendship. Love gives, but this far country toxic-love only takes and takes everything one has.

Without the restraint of the Jewish law the young man threw himself into the fast lane. With the money his father had given him he is the life and soul of the party. He has wished his father dead and left the home and the village; he has gone to a Gentile town far from all that is truth, celebrating, the lie and he has lost all of his father's money to the Gentiles. The hard work and blessing of God that had gone into the ranch at his father's hand was now in the pockets of the Gentiles, put there by his own son.

The fact is that the father's love financed the entire operation! All that was spent in buying friendship, acceptance, and false love that attempted to imitate all he had left behind was done with his father's inheritance money. The money was originally intended to be invested in the furtherance of the father's dreams and values establishing a family and celebrating love, but in the hands of the son it was now misused to create a distorted and empty substitute of the original intent.

Every breath that we breathe and every expression of our total person is given by the creator Father-God. He created us in His own image and likeness to be the delight of His love and for us to find life and meaning in His love. In our journey away from Eden we take all gifts God has given us, twisting and misusing them in the pursuit of life where there is no life or possibility of life. Only a person made in the image of God can take the gifts of God and twist and distort them to become vehicles of self-destruction!

6

Lost

. . . my son was dead. . . was lost. . .

When the young man eventually returned the father defined this period of his life by the two words: *dead. . . lost.*

Death is not something that happens to our bodies at the end of physical existence; death is what makes that happen. Death is the separation from the Creator that brings about separation of human from human and separation within the individual person. Death is terrifyingly final. When the man and the woman placed their trust in the satanic lie, they went through a door into another dimension; when they looked around, the door was gone; they could not go back; instead, they were doomed to remain in terrifying aloneness of independence where life revolved around their darkened perception of good and evil. From this time on they would live out their existence in futility searching for meaning within their own selves.

> For even though they knew God, they did not honor Him as God, or give thanks; but they became futile in their speculations, and their foolish heart was darkened. Professing to be wise, they became fools, and exchanged the glory of the incorruptible God for an image in the form of corruptible man and of birds and four-footed animals and crawling creatures. (Romans 1: 21–23)

In that day Adam invented a god, a projection of his new mindset of self-centered independence from the true God. This was a god that Satan could hide in as he pursued his passion to become the god of this world, a god through whom he could continually accuse mankind of sin that caused Adam and all his descendants to live under the condemning eye of their god and terror of his rejection and punishment. In so doing Satan fulfilled his hatred of the human that he despised as worthless trash.

Adam plunged into darkness and confusion regarding his identity and the meaning of his existence. He was dead while he lived with no exit door.

When the boy walked away from home inventing a new existence of selfish independence, death came into what he called life. In demanding his inheritance while his father lived, he had made it clear that in his mind his father was dead; he wanted to read the will and receive the inheritance that only the dead can give. Leaving home and travelling the road to the far country was rolling the stone to close the tomb. The father never ceased to love and left the door wide open for his return, but he knew the son had entered the world of the living dead.

Lost is the key word to these three parables—each is a story of something of value that has been lost—the lost coin, sheep and son being found and brought home. The word *lost* is the key to understanding this story and opens to us the heart of the father. Coupled with the word *dead,* the word *lost* can be used to describe a valued person who is presently disconnected, misplaced from the source of life and the place of belonging and is presently in a place that is irreversibly destructive, wrong, and in grave danger. It describes the state of a person who has taken the wrong path and is in a place from which there is no way back.

But at the heart of the word *lost* is the value that has been placed upon the lost item or person. It is in the same family as the word *belong*—the lost one does not belong where he is and love desperately wants him back where he belongs. This is the emphasis of Jesus' use of the word. The Pharisees would use the word to describe someone rejected and gone from sight and mind.

Jesus is not telling us how the Pharisees felt about the condition of the tax collectors but how God felt about where they were in relation to Him.

Lost is a strong word, and we use it to describe the loss of something precious—someone who has lost their wealth overnight would say that they have *"lost"* everything; someone standing in front of the ruin of a house after a tornado or fire would weep as they say they have *"lost"* their home and possessions. The sobbing parent standing at the news they have *"lost"* their child to an accident; the city-wide search for a child that is *"lost"* is accompanied with anxiety and anguish by the family. Jesus is saying that *these persons rejected by religion are of such extreme value, so precious to God that the Father sent Him, the Son, to find the lost even though it would take Him into His death to bring them home.*

Jesus is explaining in the parable why He is sitting eating with the tax collectors, why He wants to be with broken human beings. He is saying that contrary to the deep feelings of the Pharisees, these tax collectors are the kind of people He has come from the Father to resurrect from death, to make whole, to become participants in the kingdom of God. He uses the word *"lost"* because that is how both He and His Father value them and long for their return.

Jesus' use of the word is not emphasizing the state of the lost who may not know the grave danger that they in, or even know they are lost, or may in fact, even enjoying being lost! It describes the passion of the Trinity—the extreme *"so loved"* the world that resulted in Jesus the Son being here inside our humanity, sitting at table with the persons that religion abhorred. It is the reason the father is depicted running with passionate and uninhibited delight to fling his arms around the son he had lost.

The good news is not that we are sinners in grave danger *but that God counts us even in our sin as infinitely precious and will not quit until He has achieved his purpose of having us in His embrace.* Any pagan concept of God is at home with a god of condemnation, punishment, and vengeance, but the news that rocks the world and arrests us all is that the God revealed in Jesus *loves us and refuses to be God without us; He is passionately for us.*

Many who might be described as spiritual or religious are aware of a longing for God and seek for methods and disciplines to fulfill that longing, *but that longing will never be satisfied until we stand in speechless wonder at God's longing and unrelenting pursuit of us!*

That He calls us *lost* is not a word of condemnation but of definition of his love and determination to save us from living death into his embrace of *agape.*

On another occasion Jesus told a parable of a pearl merchant who searches for the ultimate pearl. Having found it he sells his entire collection to possess that one pearl. That story too is not a description of you and I seeking God but of Him seeking us and designating us as pearls of great price!

At that same time Jesus also told the story of a man finding a treasure buried in a field who sold all that he had to buy the field and claim the treasure. Jesus is the one who places such a value on us that He came where we were to take us to His Father as the delight and treasure of the Trinity.

You are his treasure and the one that He calls lost, and He will not rest until He has found you. He is the one who, having found you, throws a party and says, *"Rejoice with me, for this my son was lost and now is found."*

. . . spent everything, a severe famine occurred in that country and he began to be in need.

The lost son lived as if there was no tomorrow, drowning out the loneliness and emptiness he called life. It was all beginning to lose its luster and become a mere existence that was a parody of the life that functions in the circle of love.

The day finally came when he had spent the last penny of the inheritance money. We all come to a moment when we do not have the resources within us to pursue the phantom dancing ahead calling us and assuring us that true life, real living is just over the next hill. We have spent our lives, and there is no heart-satisfying return on our investment.

The young man's life was falling apart. Its emptiness was exposed when he had no cash to pay for the fantasy. Jesus pushed the disaster to the limit by introducing a famine co-incident with his impending poverty.

We do not experience famines in our Western world, and so we cannot imagine what Jesus was talking about. Famine means that there is absolutely no food—none! In our world today if there is a disaster or food shortage locally, help pours in from around the world. We have hard times, but we are certain that food will come from somewhere.

But to the world Jesus spoke to and the first hearers of this story, the word *famine* meant a slow and agonizing death as any meager food supplies quickly ran out. Famine meant that the far country was becoming a community of sure and certain death.

Families clung together and foraged for scraps of food, and friends shared with each other whatever could be had. But this young man is terrifyingly alone with no family, and no one shares a crust with him. In these dire circumstances the young man was forced to face the stark truth of his condition—he has never had a true friend in this place. When the last coin was gone from his purse, his friends disappeared, and even if he had money, there was no food to buy. He is alone, and in this culture that meant death.

7

Unworthy

And he went and attached himself to one of the citizens of that country, and he sent him into his fields to feed swine. And he was longing to fill his stomach with the pods that the swine were eating, and no one was giving anything to him.

His life became a continuous search for scraps of anything edible to keep him alive. He finally *attached* himself to a rancher.

The word Jesus used describes a refusal to accept rejection. It means to cling to, refuse to be shaken off, to glue, joining oneself to, pressing oneself upon another. Whatever, the rancher said he would not leave. He pushed himself on the rancher and would not go away, like a man clinging to a lifeboat and refusing to be shaken off.

In many of our big cities to stop at a traffic light is to be invaded by boys who insist on washing your car windows that do not need washing! That is the meaning of this word and is what the lonely starving boy was doing! Tell him to go away, and he insists that he stay and work for you—he will even invent a task to prove how much you need him. Realizing that he is not going away, the rancher sends him to the fields to feed the herd of pigs that wandered freely in the wild open country.

Jesus very deliberately introduced the specific work of feeding pigs into the story. The Law of the covenant was direct and simple. Leviticus 11:7 makes it clear that the pig was to be regarded as unclean and held as detestable and abhorrent, never to be eaten. To make contact with a pig or brush against one was to be regarded by the society as unclean as the pig and one must wash his body and clothes before re-entry into society. The boy was living in a Gentile city far off from such rules. The rancher was not restricted in the kind of animals that he kept.

No rancher in Israel owned pigs, and no Jew would be in close proximity to a pig and certainly would never come in contact with swine or eat pig flesh. It was the meat of abomination, the food of a broken covenant. To be close to the abominable animal in any way was to reach the absolute bottom of a broken covenant with God and family.

The pigs roamed freely in the wilderness, and the pig herder would essentially live with them, gathering their food and protecting them from predators. The pig herder was surrounded by the swine, their filth caked into his unwashed skin, their reek in the rags that he wrapped around his body.

The rancher probably saw that the boy was a Jew and knowing that a Jew would never work with pigs offered him the work expecting the man would refuse and he would be rid of him. But this young man was desperate and even with the bile rising in his throat at the thought, he went into the fields with the swine.

What the young man got out of this is hard to imagine; maybe some kind of hut for shelter and a pittance of pay or scraps from the kitchen. Whatever he received from clinging to the rancher mattered little, for the young man was slowly starving to death.

Under these conditions he would have aged in a very short time; his face gaunt, hair matted, filthy rags for clothes smelling from literally living with the pigs, eyes bloodshot, and his feet in their muck as he walked among them to feed them. And he was starving with no food coming his way; he looked with longing at the pods that he fed the pigs and longed to stuff them in his mouth, but he couldn't—to live with them was as low as he could go; to eat their food with them was too much!

The journey of this young man had ended in total and irreversible disaster. He was finished and sinking into oblivion.

Outside of and disconnected from the love of God our lives are futile; all the meanings that we may invent to give substance to life fail. They may be socially acceptable meanings or unacceptable, but all of them are futile, for we were created by God-love to be loved and to live in response to that love and only in such a response can other things and people be drawn into the meaning of life.

This was an apt picture of the men sitting at the table with Jesus. Though dressed in the best that money could buy the Pharisee and the average Israelite viewed them exactly as Jesus had described the young man. These had left their Jewish families and their faith to go to the pigs—the Roman government, the abominable Gentile—to return to their own people as collectors of the Roman taxes. As far as they were concerned, their parents and all their connection to Israel and her God were dead and buried. In exchange for their betrayal, they were given good money and all they could skim from the taxes they collected. They were the abominable to be abhorred and spat at, hated, and rejected as the Jew would a pig. If a Pharisee brushed against a tax collector he would wash his clothes and bathe to scrub the filth from his soul.

The Pharisee spat out his religious curses at tax collectors saying, *"You have broken the Law of God and are damned forever!"*

The real problem with these tax collectors (and with all of us) was not primarily a *behavior* problem but a willful turning from and breaking of *relationship* with God, a denial of the Father's love that is reflected in behavior.

Jesus publicly sat at a covenant dinner with these men, His action plainly saying *"You have broken relationship with God who is love. I am here to tell you that he loves you with unconditional love, places extreme value on you and longs to have you back home."*

Jesus is defining His mission with the story. He is drawing a line in the sand that forever separated Him from the religion of the liar that was presently in Pharisee form. Jesus' story is a declaration of war against dead religion.

Sitting with the pigs the young man *"came to himself"*; he saw himself as he truly was without excuse or blame to others. He saw the foolish decisions he had made and the arrogant life he had lived; he saw his life in shambles and he was disgusted with what he saw. He came into himself and all that he had believed to be wisdom and the best path to take in life he now called foolishness. He condemned all he had said and done, and he was filled with shame at this new seeing of himself. He was on the other side of the word *lost*.

He knew that he was disconnected, misplaced from the source of life and the place of belonging and was now in a place that was destructive, wrong. He saw himself in grave danger, as one already dead within and in process of physically dying. He admitted he had taken the wrong path, and the fear that he might never find his way back gripped him.

". . . the hired servants of my father have food that is enough and to spare while I sit here starving to death. . ."

His awakening came with a vivid memory that danced at the edge of his mind. It was a thought that would not let him go but held him. It was a vivid remembrance that lit up his present situation in sharp relief. It was a memory of the old homestead and of his father at the busiest time of the year.

His father was obviously a wealthy man with a staff of servants who lived on the ranch and were provided food and shelter throughout the year. At the springtime planting and the summer harvest they needed extra help, and temporary workers were brought in. Servants for hire would assemble in the market place in the pre-dawn hours, and local ranchers came announcing the work they had and the number of men they needed. A salary for the day would be agreed on and the men hired. There was no relationship established; they worked the day, collected their wages, and went into the night until someone needed them again. Sitting among the hogs the starving man remembered such a day and the hired men busy at the ranch. But he was drawn to and held by the sound of laughter at a luncheon his father provided for the hired men. He remembered being there, carrying the food to the table, the laughter of these simple men as they pushed away the food, unable to eat another bite. The sound of joy and well-fed men clung to his mind, a haunting melody from so far away in time and place that it might have been from another world.

It was the sound of men his father had hired for the day and might never meet again being treated like royalty with enough food to spare. Now he remembered as if it was yesterday. He had been there in the midst of the laughter, carrying the steaming plates of food, but he had not recognized the song that was all around him. He had dragged his feet with empty bored eyes resenting having to serve, not seeing the men who took the food grateful for his father's extreme kindness and generosity. Such provision of food was sheer grace; his father had no obligation to feed the hired men that passed through the ranch, certainly not with such extravagance.

The clinging memory of the sound of laughter and the warmth of father's love awakened a longing, a yearning to experience that joy even if it was as a hired man. The sound of joy was a sliver of light and hope in the midst of his hopeless darkness. It was hope that not only awakened him but called him to action to turn toward the joy. He went with a small timid hope that he could become a hired servant—he dared not hope for more.

The song from another world trumped the sight of his condition. He determined to follow the sound of the laughter and joy through the guilt, shame, and disgust that he had seen in himself.

8

I Have Sinned

I will get up and go to my father, and will say to him, "Father, I have sinned against heaven, and in your sight; I am no longer worthy to be called your son; make me as one of your hired men."

He struggled to connect with the song that called him from afar, but all he could see was his own wretched self that the light of the memory of abundance in his father's house and the sound of joyous workers had exposed. The memory of a table filled with food and surrounded with happy satisfied men who enjoyed the generous love of his father stood in stark contrast to the famine, his aching empty stomach, and the life he had in this far country. All the decisions that had seemed so right and wise when he made them now looked selfish and foolish. With the father's bountiful table still in his imagination accusers rose up within him to condemn him. "You are a loser; you are beyond the love and acceptance of anyone decent; you do not belong in anyone's family, certainly not your father's; you are not good enough to be included in his family; you are unworthy; what insanity made you think of going back there?" He could not argue with what he perceived as the facts. His lifestyle, his condition, what he looked like—everyone back at the village would all give witness to his unworthiness to ever be seen in the vicinity of his father or family member.

All he could say to his father was that he had sinned. His view of sin was limited to his stupid view of life and the actions that had followed.

"I have sinned against heaven and in your sight. . ."

Today the word *sin* has lost its edge to mean the breaking of rules—God's rules as locally interpreted by the church and society. It is understood in the context of morality and behavior. In the original language it means *to miss the mark, the original purpose or blueprint from which we were created.* This goes beyond wrong choices and lifestyles; it speaks to where that behavior originates. God revealed to Adam our human identity, the shape and form he intended for us, creating us in his own image and likeness (Genesis 1:26). Image means that Adam represented God-who-is-love to the rest of creation; it meant that he lived in a relationship of total dependence, resting in and united to God-love as the image is to the original. He was a creature in God's class.

The great lie of Satan that spawned sin was that man could break free from merely imaging God to find his destiny as an independent god, inventing his own meaning and purpose to life. This lie was activated in the eating of the tree of the knowledge of good and evil. A new system of life came into being totally other than what God had purposed, a life in which Adam would live by his own perceptions of good and evil, which were determined by his own absolutes and feelings. He had fallen from the glory of God to which he was created to live in and reflect into creation.

The young son looked at the pathway that had brought him to this moment sitting among the pigs. He summed up his life succinctly; he was guilty, totally wrong, and had played out his sin in the face of his father and family.

"I am no longer worthy to be called your son."

His calculated statement reporting how he saw himself went far deeper than his felt guilt regarding his behavior and the wrong he had done to God and man.

He had come into his core self and saw that self as wrong. He did not say that he had done things that were wrong or had made bad decisions; he addressed his essential person, his deepest identity, *I am.* From that deepest place of darkness and chaos within he declared that he was *unworthy,* which he linked not merely to his acceptance in society but to being the *son* of his father. He looked at where he came from, his birth roots, and all that bound him to his father, and in disgust declared it null and void.

Shame arises from the core of a person's very being expressed in the intense belief that they are not worthy, and are excluded from love and acceptance by God and man. The oxygen of shame is the darkness in which one hides the reasons for that controlling belief. The young man had avoided looking at that shame, hiding it behind the life of entertainment, constant activity, and friends bought with his father's money. Now it was out in the open as the darkness within had poured through his lips and spoken bitterly in self-hate.

The word he used, *worthy,* is an ancient word that described the balance of scales. He remembered going to the feed store, watching as the grain was poured into the pan, tipping the weights on the other side of the scale until the two pans balanced. That equivalency on the scales was called *worthy.*

In his self-despising eyes his lifestyle was not the equivalency of being the son of his father—or any decent father! He did not reflect the image of his father nor did he carry his values and honor into the world. He had used the inheritance money to imprint his own sinful independence on all around him. This was his final truth that in his mind declared him outside of all hope of acceptance or love.

What weights did he place on the scale to weigh his life? The only example of a perfect son who apparently obeyed and honored his father was his older brother! He was using the faulty weights to define his situation, for his elder brother was as lost to his father as he was.

He used the word *called,* which was also used in calling a person by the family name, identifying them as belonging to a certain father and family. In his estimation at the core of his person he was a homeless stranger, disconnected, with no place or part in his father's family.

He remembered the wisdom of the Law that called out the lies of the sales person who would cheat in the weights and give a false balance on the scales. In shame he put it in the center of his speech—*unworthy* a false balance. To entertain the idea of being called by his father's name meant he was a liar and a cheat.

He looked in the mirror of himself and judged himself. *Not worthy;* the words summed up and gave voice to the guilt and shame, the self-hatred that burned like acid within him. *"I am not worthy of your love, acceptance your time or concern, not worthy of your interest—I am deserving of being thrown out with the trash."*

He had lost his identity. Not knowing who he was he defined himself by his harsh rule keeping brother, his own behavior and its consequences in the circumstances he now found himself in.

Deuteronomy 32:18 describes us all:

You neglected the Rock who begot you,
And forgot the God who gave you birth.

He put together a plan of salvation that he believed would be his deliverance from the awful place that he was in. He hoped that his plan would divert his father's anger and open the possibility of becoming hired help to prove that he had reformed and was no longer the lazy-spendthrift that left the ranch. He rehearsed it to himself and told it to the pigs that nudged at his feet.

The plan that he was bringing to his father was in fact a contract that he hoped would be a solution to the standoff he perceived existed between them.

9

A Plan of Salvation

In the hell that burned in his mind he was interacting with a father that did not exist, one that was created in his own imagination. In all his thoughts the love of his father was not even considered. All his thoughts about the father and his own condition were part of his being lost. He was thinking about some solution to his situation with a mind that was broken and blind to the truth.

He could not think of facing the pain of his father's rejection, and so he made a plan that hopefully would avoid it. He would take his place as the unworthy wretch he saw that he was before his father could say it and place himself well outside of the house and home before his father could throw him out. He would go back to the village assuming the position of a rejected outsider to avoid the pain of being exposed as one not belonging to the family. He would hide behind a promise of being a better and responsible person outside of the home as a hired servant.

In his shame-controlled mind he birthed a contract that reached for his only hope of any kind of salvation; he offered himself to his father as a hired servant.

Contracts are worked out around the phrase *"If. . . then"*—*if* you do this *then* I will do that. *If* you do this work *then* I will pay you this much; *if* there is failure on either side to perform the contract *then* there will be the legal penalties, a lawsuit, and punishment. There is no relationship, no union of the parties, only the satisfaction of performance done according to the agreement.

This contract was the best hope that he could come up with. Although unworthy of being a son, he instinctively knew that the only hope he had for his wretched life was connected to his father's house. Maybe with an arm's-length employer relationship his father, seeing him working hard in the fields, could begin to accept him. It would be a kind of penance for his sinful, bad, and shameful behavior. He had arrested and judged himself believing he was reflecting the attitude and mindset of his father he did not know and determined how he must be treated and the nature of his punishment.

Sitting among the pigs, contemplating the journey home, the man was still as lost as he had always been. He was pathetic, standing as a scarecrow of a god believing he was in control of his life, satisfied with his warped ideas of salvation.

He did not dare entertain the thought of returning to the family house and home. The family home was for family members, for sons. Servants also lived on property, but hired men went to their homes at night. He would sleep where he could, in a ditch or under a bridge. He would be there in the market place in the dawn hours along with all the others for hire. His contract simply asked that whenever the father had need of hired help he would search the crowd for the face of the one that had once been his son and hire him for the day. At *least* he would get some good meals during the year!

His contract made it plain that he was not thinking of the possibility of returning to a relationship with his father. He was reaching for reformation, the chance to work and take his place in society as a moral, responsible person and attempt to be as hard-working as his brother.

In coming to himself he saw only his wretched behavior, and rejecting the self he saw, he determined to change his lifestyle. The only place he knew to begin the new life was in the call of that haunting song of joy, laughter, and the only generosity he remembered—his father's. His hope was that his father would have enough grace to relate to him at arm's length, contracting him as a hired man as needed.

His plan originated in his mind that was broken and lost; a lost mind cannot find its way out of where it is for it is part of the problem! It is lost! His problem that initiated his leaving the ranch was a false and distorted view of his father, and now his solution was based on that same twisted lie. He did not need a work program to show he had learned a lesson; that is lost thinking. He needed to accept a new truth regarding his father and his unconditional love, and trust that love as he entered into the relationship to which he was born.

Love never works from a contract arrangement, and the father never had. Love is joined in covenant, which is the polar opposite of contract. Covenant operates by *"Because. . . therefore"—because* I love you, *therefore* all that I am, is given to you with my sworn oath to which I will be faithful to death.

When mankind was blinded to the *agape* heart of God by Satan, which placed man as the point of reference for all good and meaning to life, he could no longer conceive a God of covenant love but replaced with a false god of contract. The god of contract is the pulse beat of the spiritual darkness and death. Contract was the way the Pharisees had distorted the covenant God of Israel to produce a false god of legalistic religion.

This is all that *coming to ourselves* can do. It is a self-evaluation, looking at ourselves in the mirror of things we have done or that have been done to us. We come to ourselves and determine that no one could love or accept us.

Shame sent him to the pigs where in his own mind he belonged; shame imprisoned him there and kept him from even looking in the direction of father. Shame tells us that we are irreversibly wrong at our core, not merely a person who has done wrong things.

Shame is the curse of religion that fuels and exalts as holy the belief that we are unworthy of God-love and the blessings his love longs to pour out upon us. Our intense focus on ourselves settles the matter; we are not like others who may be the beloved of God and partakers of his gifts. *We live with the pigs because we are convinced that that is all we are worthy of.*

The truth was his being lost had nothing to do with behavior. His lifestyle was the *result* of being lost. He was lost and separated from the relationship in the love and belonging with his father. He returned ignorant of the problem, believing his confessed shame and guilt was articulating the heart of the father and turning his heart toward him. His contract laid out his future life based on the misconception.

The man who turned his eyes to the road that brought him to this place was now established in his lost and dead condition, accepting it simply as the way he was. His sin against love was at full term as in his rags he would stand before his father to say that he was settled into being no longer part of the family. The story begins with his not *wanting* to be a son. He came now in self-rejection saying that he is not worthy to be *called* a son.

The extended family and the villagers that he returned to had already judged and condemned him. Should he ever return, they expected him to be punished; they would greet him as the scum of the earth, with rejection, ridicule, and shame, which would probably include a beating. They would expect the father to do as any respectable father would do, publicly humiliate the son by making him wait outside the house until summoned to the patriarch, who would order a further beating and make him a slave in the house until his lesson had been learned.

In the clothes he stood in, reeking of the abominable pigs, his constant companions, he started down the road to what he had in a distant memory once called home. He knew the rules of society and what predictably awaited him, and every step would be in fear and trepidation as he approached the village.

At this point in the story the Pharisees would applaud his groveling and attempt at lifestyle change!

It is commonly understood within the tyranny of religion that wallowing in shame and guilt is equivalent to salvation and coming to the Father! But Jesus' turn in the story horrified them.

10

Love's Vision

When he was yet a great way off his father saw him. . .

The father had never rejected the young son; he had never dismissed him from his heart but held him as one of supreme value. He held him in his heart, longing for his embrace, loving him with an unchanging love. Every day his eyes scanned the road where he had watched his boy walk away, waiting for the opportunity to hold him again and assure him of total acceptance. The villagers may have wanted revenge and punishment, but all he wanted was reconciliation. All he needed was the opportunity to give the love that dwelled in his heart.

For him to have seen the returning son when he was still a great way off, the father must have watched that road every hour, checked every passing traveler and caravan of traders for any news they may have picked up along that road. It was his constant searching love that saw the unmistakable silhouette of his son long before anyone in the village was aware of his approach.

At the sight of him his heart welled up with compassion. He dropped everything he was doing and ran towards him.

Jesus was revealing the agape heart of God in the action of the father. The one sitting with the tax collectors and in a few months going through suffering and death to find us and bring us to the longing Father was not telling a story of a father who could not wait to satisfy his hurt rage! His story had nothing to do with the demand for justice to satisfy an offended deity. The father did not welcome the boy home because his sin was punished to the father's satisfaction. The father was on a mission to satisfy his love, love that had forgiven and absorbed his son's sin. Jesus tells this story to reveal and give definition to the mission of passionate

God-love infinitely seeking reunion and relationship with the mankind he has never ceased to love.

The father of Jesus' story desired only to bring home to his arms the broken son and to make him whole and accomplish the longed for relationship.

The son had been drawn home by the remembrance of love and generosity that emboldened him to ask for the relationship of a servant! Instead he found himself in the embrace of a relationship of son with his father, drawn into love rained upon him without limit.

The young man had no plans of actually coming home to stay, only to gain the promise of employment at certain times of the year. But the opportunity had come for the father's love to do all that had been pent up in his heart for so long. He was still a great way off, far from home, not even on the property but he had come within the radius of the energy of saving love, close enough for the father to see him and come running to him.

. . . the father saw him. . .

When Jesus said that the father *"saw"* the son a great way off, He was saying more than an image of the distant young man registered in his brain. The image that the eyes register is filtered through our brain and heart for an interpretation of its meaning.

No one else in the village saw *him.* The villagers and his older brother would have seen the ghost of a man, a shadow stumbling down the road, a homeless vagabond, filthy and reeking of the abominable pigs, an outcast to be avoided—or beaten away from the village. They would see a wretched loser, barefoot and in rags who had denied his father, his people, and his God. The best he could hope for was that a stranger would look at him in pity and throw him a crust.

The tax collectors listening at the table would quickly pick up on this. No one saw them as humans, as persons; they were spat at as intruders to the peace of the village, treated and called the pariah dog that ate the filth of the village garbage. One of these tax collectors recorded the moment when he left all to follow Jesus. He records in his gospel that Jesus "*saw a man* named Matthew. . ." No one who came to his tax desk saw *a man* as they flung their money on his desk and cursed him. Jesus saw a *man* broken, in darkness, believing the lie and a slave of the liar—but Jesus saw through to the man behind the mask, a man beloved of the Father, one of the lost for whom he had come to seek and save.

Jesus could eat with tax collectors and also with the Pharisees seeing beyond their behavior, belief systems, and politics that separated human from human, into groups of *us* versus *them.* He saw the person as created to be—made in the image and likeness of God—now blitzed and broken, the screaming hurt hidden behind all walls and masks intended to hide and isolate from judging condemning fellow humans.

The father saw *him;* he did not see the behavior that left the shambles of a man in rags, but he saw his beloved son and his heart leaped for joy within him. He longed to throw his arms around him and never let go, ushering him into the family home and showering his love upon him.

The people to whom Jesus first delivered this parable lived in the awareness of the eye of their covenant God upon them. The blessing of the covenant God was placed upon them every day by the priest in the

Temple: *"The Lord bless you and keep you; the Lord make His face shine upon you and be gracious to you; the Lord lift up His countenance upon you and give you peace"* (Numbers 6:24–26).

His face shining describes the radiant, smiling face of God-the-Lover delighting in His beloved. *Lift up His countenance upon* is a phrase that describes taking special notice of another; it is the eyes locked in recognition and delight across a crowded room with a dear and looked-for friend. It is the look that speaks volumes declaring that the two persons united in a look have a special category of love and affection for each other.

The words emphasized the face of God turned *toward* them with His eye holding them in excited, delighted look of love. God was *for* them drawing them to His heart. When the blessing was spoken over the people it announced an intentional bias of God-love toward them as He smiled His favor and blessing personal to each individual upon them.

The Pharisees had created a god that was a projection of their own blinded hearts, a distorted, twisted image of the true God. They painted him with cruel steel-eyed disdain toward those not keeping the rules, seeking to find some failure to punish and damn. The thought that God had His eye upon them incited fear, anticipating his condemnation.

The first expression of this distorted perception of God was manifest when Adam and Eve, blinded by their sin, fled from His all-seeing eyes of love; through the lens of the lie they could only believe that He looked on them with rage and intent to punish.

In His every word and action Jesus dismantled the lie by revealing the true God who knows us in thought, word, and behavior as well as our unrealized potential; He knows our weaknesses and fickleness and with this total knowledge loves us unconditionally, passionately, and without limit or end.

Yet even though the eye of love looks upon us with delight, most of us secretly relate closely to this younger son. We sneak toward God feeling like a trespasser rather than a son or daughter. We are unable to entertain the thought that we have any right to think that this God-who-is-love is our home, the place of our belonging; rather we feel far from His presence, doubting that He could ever love, want, or welcome us at all. Any relationship we might hope for is a rehearsal of our contractual promises and dedications that we make to Him hoping that He will be impressed with our religious resumes. All the time we are oblivious to the eye of His passionate love, delighting to pour upon us the blessing that has been waiting for us the entire time we wandered in our blindness and confusion.

The young man, unaware of the approaching tsunami of love, was nervously rehearsing his speech as the familiar village came into view. He had no idea that even at that moment tears of joy were overflowing the eyes of his approaching father riveted upon him. He was sneaking back to the village hoping that no one saw him before he could present his business proposal to his father and he would be in line as a hired servant by tonight. He did not know that he had walked into the radar of unconditional love!

11
Compassion

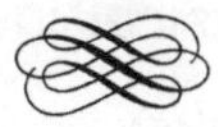

. . . was moved with compassion. . .

The shameless act of the father in running to receive the boy was fueled by compassion that literally moved him to immediate action. Jesus chose the word very deliberately. It had been used for two thousand years to describe the glory of the God of Israel. When Moses had asked to see the glory of God the words that came with that glory described Him as

> The Lord, the Lord God, compassionate and gracious, slow to anger, and abounding in loving-kindness and truth; who keeps

loving-kindness for thousands, who forgives iniquity, transgression and sin. . . (Exodus 34:6)

The word *compassion* is a very old word that originally referred to the intestines, the liver, the kidney or even the heart; it came to describe the love that wrenches the physical insides of a person. It is passionate love that glows with beautiful anger that moves to say *"I will not let my loved one continue in this condition."*

God-love is not a vague niceness that smiles benevolently from outer space! His love is defined in his acts, His salvation works on our behalf. His love never passively looks at us wishing He could help us; God-love always moves with divine energy toward us.

Compassion is God-love rising up and taking radical action to bring His love-will to the human situation, delivering and blessing the object of His love. Compassion feels with the pain of the loved one and will go to any length in its refusal to allow the hurt to continue.

The English word is made up of two Latin words, *com* meaning "with" and *passion* meaning "suffering"—it is love that suffers with the person loved.

The father united with the young man's guilt, the results of his rebellion and painful shame. His immediate willingness to endure the scorn of the village was compassion moving from his heart to the boy. Compassion was in his standing in solidarity with the ghost of a man only he could see as his son. Compassion drew the young man in a massive bear hug, embracing him and the abomination of the pig muck that clung to his clothes. He smothered him with kisses, putting his lips to the skin that reeked of the filth of far country.

In embracing him, his father had actually taken his sin and the shame of the far country in all its dimensions and made it his own. In the eyes of the gathering villagers the father was standing as his prodigal son; the son realized that potentially his father was taking all the abuse that the village would have put on him; if they would beat him, they must first fight through that bear hug that surrounded and shielded him. He was held in the father's arms where the threatened rage and mocking of the villagers could never reach him.

The father entered into the self-induced suffering of the prodigal and made it his own. The father was the one who had been sinned against and now bore the offense committed against him before the entire community; he sheltered his son in his arms one with his shame.

. . . and ran. . .

Compassion made it impossible to sedately walk to where the boy was, he had to run. Such behavior was unheard of under any circumstances. Old men simply did not run. Running involved gathering up the long robes and tying them around the waist like an awkward diaper. Such was for young men proud to show their muscular legs, but society demanded that old men hid their aging legs by walking. Running was for children and teens, but by the age of thirty the person walked as became an elder of the village; by this man's age he was expected to walk with the dignity and honor of a village elder. To run was to bring shame upon his family and upon himself. But running to meet the one the village soon realized was the rebellious son would leave everyone speechless and horrified. They would not know what to do with such scandalous behavior as the father was exhibiting. They would be embarrassed and ashamed for him, and children would laugh at the sight.

Unable to contain his relief and joy, he threw all village custom to the wind, thought nothing of the shame, gathered his robes around his waist, and ran to the faraway figure of the distant young man.

The word that Jesus used to describe the running is one that was used to describe a hundred-yard dash at the Olympics! This was urgent, a mission of prime importance to look at the face of his son and crush him in a bear-hug embrace.

By running with such unashamed delight and excitement, the father did not hide the fact that he wanted the son home! He didn't keep the young man wondering or guessing about whether he would be welcome. By running he sent a clear message that the son did not have to work to win his father's love and acceptance. He did not have to grovel or beg for a smile; his father passionately wanted him home.

Such an abandoned giving of himself placed the father in a vulnerable position, for the son he ran to could reject him. The son that he saw far off was giving no indication that he was coming home to stay or for that matter that he even wanted to see his father. He could have told the old man to go to hell! That would have been a knife through the father's heart for the second time, anguish worse than the first loss of the son. The love that Jesus defines in this father is utterly vulnerable, exposing his heart to being broken a second time.

In the far country counterfeit friends had run to meet the son because he had fistfuls of cash that he was ready to spend, but they ran from him when it was all spent! The father running to him did not make sense now, for the son had nothing to give and had earned only condemnation and rejection.

Compassion meant more than suffering with the young man's shame; the father now bestowed on him the honor of his own person in the village. Compassion meant an incredible exchange would take place. The word *reconciliation* actually means *exchange*, which is what we have vividly portrayed to us on this dirt road in the Galilee region. His wretched condition was in every way exchanged for the love and blessing of his father. He was forgiven in the deepest sense of the word. The word *forgiveness* in the New Testament means a total release from all that was past and a restoration to a relationship with his father that was greater than anything he had known before or dreamed of in his deciding to return. He came toward his father in rags but in moments would be escorted to the family table with the father's festive robe, his ring, and shoes of a son on his feet to be celebrated with the father's honor and glory.

The father could have stayed in the house removed from the situation issuing a statement of reinstatement of his son in which he forgave the son and offered him work on the ranch. He could have arranged a formal meeting in his office after the young man had bathed and found some decent clothes to discuss a period of probation and possibilities for the future. That would have been enough to shock the villagers and the first hearers of this story.

But the father's compassion scandalized every decent person listening to Jesus' story, confusing them to silence or infuriated them to rage.

The glory of the father was that he entered into and became one with the shame of his son, and that same glory was the disgust of the religious and the moral peasants in the story and of those listening.

Compassion is the anguish in the heart of God at the misery and pain He sees His children experiencing. This was the covenant God had made with Abraham and his descendants that Jesus' listeners had never understood. The word *covenant* means *to cut* and every covenant made was with cutting to produce the shedding of blood—a vivid symbol of love that would go to the death. The scandalous shame that the father gladly embraced was the cut to his heart that reached his son's heart and brought him into the family relationship for which he was born.

God the Father looked upon us with limitless and unconditional love and Jesus, the Son of God, who tells this story, is the compassion of God running to you and me to bring us home to Father's house even at the cost of his own shed blood.

12

This Son of Mine

. . . embraced and kissed him. . .

The father, driven by compassion, burst on the returning son like a volcano erupting. He flung his arms around the boy and began to smother him with kisses between laughter and tears. The son was prepared for a very different kind of return to the village and his father and was totally unprepared for this explosion of love, forgiveness, and welcome. He did not know what to do except receive the hug and kisses that would not cease.

The son, held within the arms of his father and pulled into his chest, was engulfed in the aromatic oil that the father had, like all other Israelites, anointed his head with that morning. The father's face, beard, and robe all carried that unique smell of father and home. To be buried in the folds of the robe and to feel his father's face wet with his tears against his and to feel his repeated kisses combined to give one message: he was loved! Forgiven! Accepted! All guilt and shame for what he had done was carried away in that embrace. From the depths of the bear hug of love he could face the village with confidence and boldness knowing that the father's love restored, affirmed, and established him as a full family member.

Something happened when the son took in what was happening. The young man saw and felt the full force of his father's love—a love that he had never known or conceived of even though he had been raised in the midst of it. He was in the middle of the fierce love event. He saw the shame the father had willingly taken by his mad dash to embrace him. For the first time in his life he looked love in the face and saw the extent to which the father's compassion would go to receive him; he saw how much his father wanted him.

The contract promises made in the far country to being a morally responsible worker now looked hollow and empty, a worm-eaten foundation for any relationship to his father. In the far country, working as a hired man for his father was his way of salvation and a self-imposed punishment for his behavior, proof of his sincere desire to change. Becoming a hired man was his only hope of some kind of acceptance and the basis of any future relationship to his father.

In the light of the outpouring of love the speech outlining the contract that had been rehearsed these many days was no longer applicable; he began to give it, but he stopped short of the contract offering himself as a man for hire. Becoming a hired man was the lynchpin that held together his hoped-for future. Stopping short of saying it meant that he had a radical change of mind and redirection of his hope of the future. He retained the sight of himself as a person who has sinned and was unworthy of any place in the family, but it dawned on him that the father saw the same person but had a radically different opinion of him. The stunning truth washed over him; his father loved him with a tenacious love just as he was.

In that moment he abandoned the contract—it died in his mouth. The passionate love of his father became the new foundation of the relationship that now began to take shape in his wondering mind. Love had revealed the cold ugliness of contract and killed it.

A contract cannot live in the active presence of covenant love. In the arms of forgiveness and acceptance the idea of becoming his father's hired man was redundant and foolish.

This was not merely feeling sorry for what he had done or a desperate attempt to conjure up a belief that the father would be generous. Such would have not constituted reconciliation but a dead mental faith in his own faith. What we see here is radical mind change—an exchange of his own thoughts, opinions, and intentions for his father's thoughts, opinions, and intentions. For the first time he saw his father as he truly was and at the same time saw himself as he truly was in his father's eyes; he saw and yielded to the father's thoughts and desires for him. In that moment he saw and believed in the father's love and rested in the faith of his father that he was indeed his son restored to him.

From here on the foundation of his relationship to his father was the father's love and faith. Love won, and the son stopped struggling against his acceptance, abandoned his contract, and yielded to the love of the father.

This is true repentance—a radical change of mind created by the revelation of God-love; we believe and trust the love of the Father that is revealed to us in Jesus.

When the son came with his contract, he believed that he had the situation and any future relationship with his father firmly under his control. The outpouring of the father's unconditional love made it plain that the son had never had control. The initiative of the relationship had always been in the hands of the father, and any future relationship would be established on his love alone. The only part the son can contribute is to surrender to that love.

He surrendered and dared to trust his father's love even though it was beyond his comprehension.

He realized that he had never known his father; the images he had held of his father did not fit the reality happening in his embrace. He surrendered, not as a conquered loser but as one who opened his heart to yield with joy to such a father's love and the life that opened before him. On that road he opened to the possibility of a relationship with his father that was outside the realm of his wildest imagination. He accepted his being beloved of the father; he accepted his acceptance and relaxed into allowing father-love to pursue his goal.

The boy found his true identity in the eyes of father's love—the same eyes that had seen him from afar. The young man's own dark self-identity unraveled; the assembling villagers' assessment of him was stopped and rebuked—the father and only the father defined him, declaring him to be his beloved son.

But the father said to his slaves, "Quickly bring out the best robe and put it on him, and put a ring on his hand and sandals on his feet; and bring the fattened calf, kill it, and let us eat and be merry; for this son of mine was dead, and has come to life again; he was lost, and has been found."

These words constitute the heart of the story. Jesus is answering the questioning Pharisees as to why He sat at table in a meal of solidarity with the outcasts of society. The story now made it plain with the astonishing announcement that these untouchables were not only forgiven but were lost sons that Jesus had come to find and bring home to the Father.

The father's servants had followed their master's mad run down the road and now stood watching in a bemused wonder at what was happening before their eyes. He ordered them to serve the ragged man in front of him by bringing his own best robe and shoes and dress him while he placed a signet ring on his finger. He sent others to prepare for a feast of celebration for the entire village.

They looked at him stunned and amazed, and he answered their unspoken question with *"for this son of mine. . ." For* or *because* gave the reason for his astonishing behavior. The robe a person wore, whether they wore shoes or not, and the ring on their finger all spoke in that culture to a person's identity. The gifts were the symbols of what he now plainly states: *". . . for this son of mine was dead and is alive, was lost and is found."* The servants must do the unthinkable and serve and dress the boy *because* he is the father's son.

Everyone in the village had a reason to reject the boy; no one would give the boy a look, let alone a reference! But the father had a totally different evaluation that silenced all others. He announced for all to hear *"this son of mine."*

This son of mine. . . the father designates him emphatically as his son, one born of him, alive with his life, and belonging to his family. He was not an outcast but one who belonged to his father and shared in all that the father had.

The son was stunned, hardly taking in what he heard. It was like a wild dream, an insane flight of the imagination, the last thing that he expected to hear. But it was not a dream—it was the affirming witnessing voice of the father that resonated in his heart. In these words we are privy to the most private and intimate moment between the father and the son. Yet at the same time the words were an announcement to the entire village implying that they were to take the father's lead and treat and respect this man as his son.

The father's words opened up a new world. The young man had returned to be in his father's employ. An employer of a hired servant expected the servant to give respect, to fulfill the terms of their contract, and to give a day's work in exchange for wages. The relationship ended at the end of the day when each went their separate ways. With this as his only hope the young man had returned down the road to home. Instead he heard the words *"this son of mine"* that introduced a new and undreamed of life.

A father loves his children to life, nurtures them, and welcomes them into his heart to share his life as he participates in their joys and tears, their laughter and play. *Father* means the provider of all that is needed to live; he is the one who watches over and protects his family. He is the affirming voice about their identity and destiny as family members and blesses them into adulthood. A *father* is never satisfied until he knows that his children fully know and receive his love for them and reciprocate in loving him.

This son of mine. . . the words of the father awakened the son to his true identity at the core of his being. The declaration created assurance so strong that he could accept his acceptance in the family and the restoration of the lost relationship to the father. He is drawn to respond in trust and obedience to the father's word.

The word Jesus used for *father* in the original language is *abba*, the word of family intimacy. It was the first word the child learned and was used throughout life between father and children. It is essentially equivalent to our English word daddy, dad or poppa. When I lived in Brooklyn, I would travel the subway and watch as the toddlers of the Jewish families would jump on their father's lap and tug on their beards saying, "Abba, Abba!"

Jesus introduced us to this most intimate relationship with God. He always called God his *abba* and invites us to share with him this same relationship. We are called to leap with delight into the lap of God-who-is-love as His beloved children and hear Him say to each one of us *"you are my son, my daughter."*

Jesus defined eternal life, the life that he came to give us as being awakened to, knowing God as Abba:

> And this is eternal life that they may know Thee (Abba), the only true God, and Jesus Christ whom Thou hast sent. (John 17:3)

The word *know* is not to know about but to know by personal observation and experience; it is the knowing of the heart, our core being not merely knowing about, an abstract intellectual knowledge.

We are more than what our parents and family or peers say of us; we are more than the externals that prop us up in our presentation to our world. It is the word of the Father, our Abba, that defines us, declaring us his child in our union with Jesus. His affirmation silences all other contradictory words.

Listen to the Father's faith in the achievement of his own love as he defines you and declares your identity.

> For you have not received a spirit of slavery leading to fear again, but you have received a spirit of adoption as sons by which we cry out, "Abba! Father!" The Spirit Himself bears witness with our spirit that we are children of God, and if children, heirs also, heirs of God and fellow heirs with Christ. . . (Romans 8:15–17)

The purpose from before the foundation of the cosmos was always that we should be his children who sit at his table and open our hearts to being his beloved and to rest in that love.

This son of mine. . . Remember that the son who had left the far country to return down the road toward his father's house was, in his mind, as far away from his father as he had ever been. He has said that he was no longer worthy to be called his father's son and desperately hoped that he will be counted worthy to walk on the family property as a hired man. This was his hope as his father embraced him. His pathetic prepared speech bitterly declared intentional separation from father and home.

It was at *this* moment when the son believed himself to be beyond the inclusion and acceptance into the father's life or place in the family. It was at this point of hopeless despair and incredible sadness that he heard the father's voice above all the voices in his head and the united voices of his brother and the villagers, the voice declaring him to be *this son of mine.* Spoken to him at his lowest moment, there could never be a doubt in his mind as to his unconditional acceptance.

13

Found Alive

. . . for this son of mine was dead, and has come to life again; he was lost, and has been found.

. . . W*as lost and has been found. . .* The father is not in denial as to his son's past. He had walked the road out of a terrible wilderness filled with grave danger. The father summed up those years as *lost* describing the ache and longing in his own heart for the return of his son. In using the word *lost* he was underlining the extreme value that he placed on the ragged man who stood awkwardly in front of him.

It is the same designation that Jesus had introduced into the two previous stories of the lost coin and lost sheep. The sheep was described as lost because it had value to the shepherd; it was worth hard-earned money, and he had invested long hours in the well-being of the sheep. It was not a wild creature but an owned and valued animal, and that value was high enough for the shepherd to risk his own life in going into the wilderness to bring the sheep out.

The value the father placed on the son was infinitely more than a rancher would place on a sheep. If a village was called to rejoice over a sheep being found, how much more should it rejoice over a son being held in his father's arms after having been lost in the far country.

He had told the story of the coin that was lost. It was a small coin of little monetary value, but it was part of a set of ten coins probably held together on a string that hung around her neck given to her by her husband at their marriage. The necklace string had broken, and the coin was lost somewhere in the darkness and dirt of the house.

The fact that it was lost did not diminish its value. The stamp on its face identified its worth even though no one could see it in the darkness. It being missed from the necklace screamed its value even louder than when it hung around her neck. It had to be found because of the unseen value proclaiming the covenant love of her husband.

If she called her friends and neighbors together to celebrate its being found, how much more should they celebrate when this son bound to the father in covenant love was back in the binding tie of that love.

. . . for this son of mine was dead, and has come to life again. Something new is introduced in these three stories. The sheep and the coin had been lost and then found, but the father says his son had not only been lost but *dead* and was now *alive.*

Dead is far more horrific than lost. The sheep had been lost but not dead, and although a coin could be lost, it could never be described as dead. *Dead* could only be used to describe the terrible separation that had come between father and son. He was a valued son but also a son who did not know or walk in relationship with his father.

An animal's life such as the sheep's was an existence, but humans were created to be infinitely more than merely existing. Made in the image of God we were to exist in the triune love of God and each other. Real life that Jesus called eternal life is not merely extended existence, but it is in this here-and-now moment knowing the love of God our Father as it has been revealed in Jesus.

> And this is eternal life that they may know Thee (Abba), the only true God, and Jesus Christ whom Thou hast sent. (John 17:3)

Death describes separation from the life that is dwelling in the *agape* love of the Father through Jesus the Son in the fellowship of the Spirit. The son had been separated from his father and from his family in the village. He was separated from his own true self, not knowing his identity, having lost his moorings and drifted into the death of a great unknowing.

But now he is *alive.* The word Jesus placed in the mouth of the father described resurrection from the dead. Resurrection is not merely life from the dead but life from the dead that is of a different kind to the life that had ceased and buried. It introduces a life that cannot die that transcends all that was understood by life prior to resurrection. It is a word of miracle, for death announces the end with no way back; resurrection announces not only a miraculous reversal of that verdict but a way forward into life that, although a continuation, is utterly new and different.

The young man stood before the father and the village—the same son that had left and yet been reborn to a relationship with the love of his father that he had never known or dreamed of.

14

Abundant Life

His far-country hope of a good meal a few times a year had been swallowed up in the reality of his newfound identity. He was now immersed into something infinitely greater. He was not made a hired servant to receive such bounty once or twice a year or even once a month. He was announced as a son in the father's house to have share of ownership of such abundance and to join his father in dispensing out of it more than enough to spare for others who crossed their path.

This is not merely the story of the young man being forgiven but of his eyes being opened to discover his true identity as the father's son. The servants, the robe, the shoes, and the ring are all symbols of his new identity. These items speak of his true self as they announced to the village that he must now be received as the son of his father. The far-country identity that he had given himself after his look into the abyss of his broken self unraveled; the villagers' assessment of him was stopped and rebuked—the father and only the father defined who the son truly was.

There are countless believers who look at their past behavior and grovel, hoping for but never sure of forgiveness and acceptance. Their view of themselves is rooted in their past and all that is wrong with them. The Father revealed by Jesus does not talk about our past that has been crucified, dead, and buried with Christ. He is not obsessed with sin but consumed with passion to establish us in our new life as his resurrected and restored sons and daughters. Our true identity is not found in struggling with sin but developing our new life in Christ.

The Spirit convicts not that we might grovel before a god we are terrified to approach but convinces us that we are living far below our privilege of what the love of God has prepared for us that is beyond our wildest dreams or possible for our minds to imagine.

His conviction leads us to realize that the behavior of the far country does not reflect who we truly are and that it must be recognized as dead and buried with Christ and our life choices aligned to our true self alive in the resurrected, ascended Christ. He opens our mind to the new possibilities of the abundance the Father presses upon us. He does not emphasize who you are *not* but who you *are* and who you are *becoming* in the embrace of the Father.

The son had returned thinking and planning a meeting that focused on sin, failure, and everything *he was not;* the father's love announced his true identity, everything he *truly was.* God does not focus on what is *wrong* with us but on who he has made us and where he is taking us, the beloved children that we are.

The new covenant that Jesus initiated does not call us to the hired man mentality, earning an occasional blessing by performance of endless religious duties. In the Old Testament the presence of the Spirit the dispenser of all grace, and blessing came *upon* persons at certain times for a specific work. The Spirit was *with* these believers, but Jesus introduces the New Covenant as being far superior when he said that the

Spirit who had been *with* them would continue to be *with* and *upon* us but now *in* us, permanently dwelling and sharing our lives. We do not receive an occasional feast but live in the middle of abundance with enough to spare.

You are now on a journey discovering how amazing and beautiful you are in the eyes of the Father. You are now vulnerable to the love of God—you will learn to feel that love.

The young man was overwhelmed by the ferocity of his father's love. The unconditional God-love is terrifying when we first become aware of Him. God-love cannot be controlled; there is nothing that we can do to make him love us. He was already passionately pursuing us when we became aware of Him. We cannot appeal to his pity to make him feel sorry for us, for he is already moved with compassion toward us before we knew him. God-love always throws all the religious control freaks off balance and blows away their speeches.

The Holy Spirit is God running to us in unashamed delight and excitement, communicating that he wants us. He is the divine invasion upsetting all our religious plans and sweeping us into the arms of His love's purpose for us. He never compels, controls, or manipulates us; He makes us willing by His love.

In that moment he was speechless with nothing to say except to accept his acceptance. He received the robe, ring, and shoes without the pushback of "You can't do this to me—I am not worthy!" His receptive silence was that of one who has surrendered to love and will walk into the party as the one who is his father's son.

15

The Father's Robe

But the father said to his slaves, "Quickly bring out the best robe and put it on him."

The father and son did not proceed to the ranch immediately to greet the entire household and be presented to the village in the rags of the far country. The father ordered the servants to *bring* the robe to where they were, and he was robed out on the road where his father's love found him. The household and the villagers would not see him as he was when his father found him; that was love's secret buried between the two of them for "love covers a multitude of sins."

God does not hang out our dirty laundry for all to see, making us pay for sin by humiliating us. His love is sheer kindness and gentleness, even hiding our sins from those who would delight to condemn and accuse us. He took the guilt and shame and wrapped the prodigal in the robes of acceptance and honor.

"The blood of Jesus Christ God's Son cleanses us from all sin"; as soap goes through every fiber of the sweater and carries the dirt out and away so we are cleansed, and all that belongs to the far country is gone. And, *"what God has cleansed let no man call common."*

The father said, *". . . bring the best robe."* He was undoubtedly referring to his own robe that hung in his closet reserved for high and holy days of celebration reflecting the father's most joyous and honored moments. The word Jesus used to describe this robe is used in Isaiah 61:3: *"a mantle of praise."*

As we have said previously the *best robe* spoke of the identity of the person who wore it. In our culture clothes speak of the latest fashion or fad, and shirts sometimes identify us with a sports hero or a message we want to be conveyed. In the culture of Jesus' day clothes defined a person's identity and state of mind; they literally wore their heart. Clothes defined one's place in the society; they told whether you were angry, in mourning, or attending a joyous feast. If you were a leper with contagious disease, there were clothes for that too! When Jesus said that the father put his own best robe on the boy, he was announcing the identity he was giving the son.

The father knew well where his son had been; his life story was written clearly in the rags he wore and the absence of shoes. But although he saw his son's outward appearance, he dressed him in accord with the truth that love knew him to be, the son he delighted in.

It was the best robe the father had in his closet although as far as the young man was concerned any clothes would have been eagerly accepted. A second-hand robe would have excited him!

The robe the father gave was not to cover the embarrassment of the boy's true condition; it declared to all who saw him his true identity. Under that robe was not a ragged homeless loser but in truth and in fact his beloved and honored son.

To put on clothes in this culture meant that the clothes described who the wearer truly is. The imagery is even used of God in Isaiah 59:17:

And He put on righteousness like a breastplate,
And a helmet of salvation on His head;
And He put on garments of vengeance for clothing,
And wrapped Himself with zeal as a mantle.

In this imagery the Lord is not hiding who he is under clothes that mask him! He is not pretending to be someone He is not! Quite the reverse: He is truth and absolute reality, and his *"putting on"* is vivid imagery describing his acting in a certain way to reveal His true identity and who He really is.

The imagery is used to picture the reality of God's gift of salvation, the bestowing of his righteousness. Everyone listening to Jesus would be aware of the Scriptures that described salvation in this way, especially the Pharisees. One such Scripture is Isaiah 61:10:

I will rejoice greatly in the Lord,
My soul will exult in my God;
For He has clothed me with garments of salvation,
He has wrapped me with a robe of righteousness.

The prophet Zechariah had spoken in similar language to Joshua the high priest:

> Now Joshua was clothed with filthy garments and standing before the angel. And he spoke and said to those who were standing before him saying, "Remove the filthy garments from him." Again he said to him, "See, I have taken your iniquity away from you and will clothe you with festal robes." Then I said, "Let them put a clean turban on his head." So they put a clean turban on his head and clothed him with garments, while the angel of the LORD was standing by. (Zechariah 3:3–5)

Isaiah had spoken of the Messiah as exchanging our spirit of despair and depression for the garments of praise (Isaiah 61:10).

In the epistles we are commanded to "put on" and "put off" certain behaviors. These phrases are specific to describe the putting on and off of clothes. The verses speak of putting on the clothes of a lifestyle that is in accord with who we believers truly are in Christ. Our coming to know and live in the love of God is described in terms of a wardrobe full of clothes that reflect divine love that we are to *put on* and so perfectly express our new identity in Christ. We are to align our behaviors with the person we now are. We put on the lifestyle not to *become* the beloved but because we *are* and the new clothes truly express our identity. In the same passages we are commanded to *put off,* or a better translation is to fling from us, throw away, discarding with disgust the behaviors that no longer reflect our new true identity.

Understand what was happening on the road in Jesus' story in the light of these Scriptures:

> . . . that you be renewed in the spirit of your mind, and *put on* the new self, which in the likeness of God has been created in righteousness and holiness of the truth. (Ephesians 4:23–24)

> But now you also, *put them all aside:* anger, wrath, malice, slander, *and* abusive speech from your mouth. Do not lie to one another, since you laid aside the old self with its *evil* practices, and

> have *put on* the new self who is being renewed to a true knowledge according to the image of the One who created him (Colossians 3:8–10)

> . . . bond slaves to be subject to their own masters in everything, to be well-pleasing, not argumentative, not pilfering, but showing all good faith that *they may adorn* the doctrine of God our Savior in every respect. (Titus 2:9–10)

The Message paraphrase captures the meaning of the passage:

> Don't lie to one another. You're done with that old life. It's like a filthy set of ill-fitting clothes you've stripped off and put in the fire. Now you're dressed in a new wardrobe. Every item of your new way of life is custom-made by the Creator, with his label on it. All the old fashions are now obsolete. . . From now on everyone is defined by Christ, everyone is included in Christ. So, chosen by God for this new life of love, dress in the wardrobe God picked out for you: compassion,

> kindness, humility, quiet strength, discipline. Be even-tempered, content with second place, quick to forgive an offense. Forgive as quickly and completely as the Master forgave you. And regardless of what else you put on, wear love. It's your basic, all-purpose garment. Never be without it. (Colossians 3:19–24)

To wear the father's robe conveyed all that it symbolized. The robe around his shoulders was his entrance into father's house to be and to learn how to act in accord with the robe he wore. For him to wear the robe immediately upon his showing up on the road was horrifying to the philosophy of the Pharisees. If they could conceive of his ever wearing the robe of his father, it would be only after the young man proved himself and earned his right to wear the robe.

But the way of father's house was the polar opposite. The father's first order of business was to sweep the broken man into his arms of love, robe him, and declare him to be his son, and then in the midst of hilarious joy learn to live that out.

16

Shoes and a Ring

". . . put a ring on his hand"

The father placed his own ring on the young man's hand. It was a signet ring that bore the seal of the family. The ring was a visible and tangible symbol of his identity as a member of the family. When impressed in wax or clay it would leave the imprint of the family seal and all the honor and authority of the family name stood behind that seal.

The signet ring was the father's word declaring him his son publicly displayed on his finger. It was the father's permission to act like his son, the *yes* to his status and authority in the family. The signet ring on his finger was his qualification to act and further the father's purposes in the village. From the placing of the ring on his hand he could draw upon the worth and abundance of his father in every situation in which he found himself.

Signet rings are mentioned throughout the Scriptures and were used as part of daily life. They varied in size, shape, and beauty; depending on the wealth of the family they might be jeweled, but they were always treasured possessions. Certain items worn by the high priest of Israel were likened to such a ring as this.

"With the work of an engraver in stone, like the engravings of a signet. . . you shall set them in settings of gold" (Exodus 28:11).

Worn on the finger, the family signet ring silently announced the identity of the wearer. It was the ring of belonging, identifying the wearer with a specific family. The ring was the guarantee that the wearer would receive the honor and respect that was due the family whose signet it bore.

The Genesis story of the bringing of Joseph out of prison to be honored by the Pharaoh includes his being given the ring of the royal family that all might know that he is to be treated with the same respect as the Pharaoh.

> Then Pharaoh took his signet ring off his hand and put it on Joseph's hand; and he clothed him in garments of fine linen and put a gold chain around his neck. (Genesis 41:42)

The ring carried the power and authority of the family whose seal it bore. It carried the authority of the presence of the person who owned the ring even if they were physically absent or the ring was given to another to be worn as the owner's representative. It was understood that the treatment expected to be given to the owner of the ring was to be given to the one who wore it.

A letter with the seal of the king's ring at the bottom of the document meant that the words in the letter carried the power and authority of the king himself.

> "You yourself write a decree concerning the Jews, as you please, in the king's name and seal it with the king's signet ring; for whatever is written in the king's name and sealed with the king's signet ring no one can revoke." (Esther 8:8)

It was the way in which purchases were made and signatures signed. The ring given to the son was the father's, and so, in effect, he was handing to the son his own status, respect, and authority in the village; he was giving him the key to his bank account and his credit in the community. Based on his own track record the son would have no status or credit, and backed by the testimony of the elder brother, he would be ostracized by the townsfolk who believed he should have been beaten and punished. But the ring changed all of that. Now he had the name and respect of his father and his authority to sign for whatever he needed in his return to society.

God-love has not only embraced us and declared us his sons and daughters, but the Holy Spirit is the witnessing ring declaring our true identity. He not only witnesses within us but reveals to us the authority of the name of the Lord Jesus bringing his presence into every situation.

Love has included us in the family of Christ and given us His name that we might, in his authority, stand against the world's darkness and bring his salvation. We have been given boldness to fellowship to ask of the Father as Jesus. We walk into every day in His name enabled and strengthened by the Spirit to be all that love commands us to be and do with joy and thanksgiving.

". . . and shoes on his feet. . ."

In Israel everyone wore shoes that were much like the sandals of our Western world. In hard times people would let go of the luxuries of life, but they held on to their sandals until they were worn out and could not be repaired. One's identity was bound up with their shoes; they were the symbol of a free person with a place in family and society. A shoeless person was one who had fallen to the lowest poverty level of society, or they were a slave.

Placing shoes on the young man's feet identified him as the son of his father and no man's slave.

Significantly when a conquering army took captives, they removed the shoes of their prisoners, symbolizing that they were now captives and slaves of the conquerors. Release from captivity and slavery was marked by the putting on of shoes—celebrating that they were now free persons (Isaiah 20:1–5; 2 Chronicles 28:15).

Deuteronomy tells us that the shoes of the Israelites did not wear out in their wilderness journey. It is a simple statement that describes the love of God that gave them the silent miracle reminding them to celebrate every day that they were free from slavery and to walk as his people.

Without shoes the young man would have been identified as the lowest slave of a Gentile pig farmer in the far country; for the father to say that a shoeless man was his son would have been an oxymoron and brought shame on the family. He who came back to his father to be a hired servant, little more than a slave, now finds himself with servants kneeling at his feet to put on sandals, mutely declaring that he was no one's slave but a free man, the beloved son of the father.

God-love has set us free from all bondage to the powers of darkness and lies; we are no longer slaves of sin or the commands of the Law. It is a not freedom to remain lost and separated. It is freedom that carries with it a union with God-love; set free in order to fulfill the meaning of our creation in being the functional sons and daughters of God.

In Jesus a new kind of slavery came into existence. It begins with knowing that we are limitlessly loved, the delight of the Father. Knowing that we are His sons and daughters, members of His family, sharing His life and enjoying relationship with Him, we respond by freely and joyfully serving Him. Our first relationship is that of children of God, not servants. Only when we walk free in His love can we freely choose to serve Him in love responding to love.

> And because you are sons, God has sent forth the Spirit of His Son into our hearts, crying,

"Abba! Father!" Therefore you are no longer a slave, but a son; and if a son, then an heir through God. (Galatians 4)

17

Rejoice!

". . . and bring the fattened calf, kill it, and let us eat and be merry; for this son of mine was dead, and has come to life again; he was lost, and has been found." And they began to be merry.

The father and son, now robed, shoed, and with the family ring on his finger moved through the assembled villagers to the celebration party that was being prepared back in the family home. The villagers joined in the feast, celebrating the one that they would have planned to beat; they decided that a feast of rejoicing was a better idea than a lynch mob! The calf that had been separated from the herd and fattened for such a time of extreme celebration had been slaughtered and was already roasting. Music had the villagers dancing throughout the property, and the son on the arm of his father was escorted as the honored guest into the festivities.

It was hardly an hour before that the son had been timidly coming to the vicinity of what used to be home, expecting a beating and rejection. This one who would have counted the promise of being a hired hand a prize was now in the midst of a party that celebrated his return.

The previous two parables have the shepherd and the woman having found that which was lost call their neighbors to "Rejoice with me for I have found that which was lost." The feast and festivities that father and son now go to parallels the rejoicing of the previous stories. The word *rejoicing* in the language of Jesus meant to spin around and leap in the air for joy! Jesus uses this extreme word to describe the joy in the hearts of those who found the lost sheep and coin and now, the son beloved of the father. The call in the parables is "Rejoice with me" and "Let us be merry"; the father was saying, "Join with me in my uncontained excitement!" Jesus is describing the unbounded and uninhibited joy and delight of Abba God at the securing of one person into the experienced knowledge of his love. Shocking as it is to the religious Pharisees, holiness is described as a party expressing extreme joy.

God our Abba is not a solemn judge always on the edge of being annoyed and irritated with us. He is Abba, laughing and dancing for joy that we are home, inviting us to leap in the air with him. Peter calls this "Joy unspeakable and full of glory."

The son was caught up in the rejoicing. His was not merely joy that he was home in a way he had never dreamt; he was rejoicing in his father's joy of love fulfilled and triumphant. The joy of the father was to look at his son and know that he was home; all the music, dancing, and feasting could not describe the joy in his heart at the sight of his son seated beside him. The son's assurance of his right to be there was the reflection of the radiant smile and laughter on his father's face. The delight of his father was the son's permission to be bold in believing and acting as the celebrated son of his father.

It echo's the description of restoration in the Psalms:

When the Lord brought back the captive ones of Zion,
We were like those who dream.
Then our mouth was filled with laughter,
And our tongue with joyful shouting;
Then they said among the nations,
"The Lord has done great things for them."
The Lord has done great things for us;
We are glad. (Psalm 126:1–4)

Thou hast turned for me my mourning into dancing;
Thou hast loosed my sackcloth and girded me with gladness;
That *my* soul may sing praise to Thee, and not be silent.
O Lord my God, I will give thanks to Thee forever. (Psalm 30:11–12)

The son discovered that the father was not affected by the poverty and famine that ravaged the far country! He had not run out of cash when he divided the inheritance, and he now lavished his wealth on the boy. Religion teaches us that holiness is solemnity, groveling, and self-abasement, but Jesus is defining it as extreme joy and abundance clothed in favor and surrounded by blessing.

This was not an event on the road after which they went their separate ways to talk about that moment forever. The event was only the beginning of a relationship in which the father welcomed the son into his home and honored and celebrated him. Jesus pointedly said that they *began* to be merry with no record that they stopped after the party ended.

The life that Jesus gives is not to be thought of as an isolated event in which a decision is made to settle what happens after death. The event of meeting with the love of God is the gateway into a new relationship with God. It is a radically new way of living, a new dimension of life that we settle into and live out in this world.

Jesus emphasized this by calling our life in relationship with Him an abiding or remaining, staying, settling into our new home in the heavenly realm. It is a new way of life that is aligned to the Father and the Son with and in whom we live out our lives in the earth.

The Holy Spirit is our teacher, guide, and coach in becoming increasingly aware and at home in this home that is characterized by the Father's joy and delight in us. The God-love is not a general niceness smiling at us. God-love is the fierce and determined love that will not rest until He has brought us to the full knowledge and participation in our relationship and union with the Trinity for which we were created.

The father's joy had filled the village with the sounds and smells of rejoicing, of roast beef and community dancing. The son sat down to a meal he had not seen in years with the love and acceptance he had never allowed himself to know. He does not sit with a stingy king or with a manipulating businessman but with the love that only gives in abundance, exceeding greatness, grace that abounds much more, and an agenda that was simply rejoice with his father that his joy might be full. The returned son could only accept without effort, sweat, or anxiety the love being showered upon him.

As we have seen, the psalmist said this salvation causes us to be as one who dreams. A dream does not follow the logic of our minds but operates in another dimension that is akin to imagination. It is the world of seeing what we cannot presently put words to; it is holding pictures of the potential, the possible of the life we are presently only tasting. Joy does not come from external happenings or gains. Joy is rooted in that which can never be lost—if the cause of joy can be lost, then it is not the joy that Jesus is speaking of. This joy is internal, a fruit of the Spirit found in the moving toward the potential and possible of God-love in our life and experience. Whatever external events may be taking place, we live in the joy that our true life is rooted in the Father's love now present with us in whatever the moment holds. The father was escorting his son as the heir he saw him to be, a vision that presently was beyond the son to comprehend.

Looked at through eyes of intellect and logic, the Gospel seems like a fantasy that is too good to be true. In a daze we rest in its incredible news, respond and trust in the character and love of God revealed to us in Jesus. Scripture tells us that this life falls into the category of eyes that have not seen nor ears heard nor conceived by the heart of man the things that the Father has laid up for those who love him—a life that the Spirit now begins to enlighten us in, teach us, and guide us into. It points to a fullness of union with God that holds within it possibility that is beyond our asking or thinking; that is the dimension of dream and imagination.

Jesus consistently portrayed the kingdom of God as a feast. The kingdom of God is joy—the joy of the Spirit over who you are, the beloved of God.

They began to be merry. . . The party and the rejoicing would characterize the rest of their life together; they *began to be merry,* but Jesus gave no indication that they would turn out the lights and the party would be over! The rejoicing would define the years ahead when father and son working together on the ranch would be merry together in all that they did. There is no drudgery, sighing, or weariness in the Father's house. The sorrow and sighing flee, and we enter into rest from labor to work in His strength that renews us as we work.

The word that is used throughout the Scripture to describe this relationship of love is *righteousness.* The word *righteousness* describes the living out of the right relationships of covenant love. It describes covenant partners walking in and fulfilling the terms of a covenant relationship. It has nothing to do with a perfect behavior record. The action of the father in bestowing love was fulfilling his covenant relationship to this one who was bound to him by blood, a love not based on earning or deserving but on a life-love that was expressed in *son of mine.* The righteousness of the son was to believe the righteousness of the father and enter into a relationship of trusting his love.

It is important to note that the father had no interest whatsoever in a report of the son's previous life either as a confession or as the backdrop of the promise to improve it by assuming moral responsibility. All he wanted was the boy to trust his love and enter into relationship with his love—that is righteousness.

This is not the story of the son achieving his end of persuading the father to believe in his promise of self-reformation; it is the story of the father persuading the son to believe that he is loved, accepted, and resurrected to a relationship that originated in the father's heart of covenant love.

18

Religious Rage

Now his older son was in the field, and when he came and approached the house, he heard music and dancing. And he summoned one of the servants and began inquiring what these things might be.

But there was something else happening in the vicinity of the music, dancing, and feasting celebrating love's longing fulfilled. The older brother after a day of work on the ranch was coming across the fields anticipating a bath, dinner, and bed before heading out to do the same in the next morning. As he came closer to the house he heard the music and sounds of laughing people, and the smell of roasting beef was in the air.

It is interesting that in his story Jesus has this brother hearing what the younger one had heard in his memory. They both walk toward the ranch drawn by the sound of music and joy. The younger one had come wanting a piece of that action while the older comes with rising consternation at what has taken place without his knowledge.

As he came closer he saw one of the ever-present children of the village (a better translation than servant) and summoned him, demanding information about what was going on. The words used by Jesus suggest one speaking down to an inferior, one who knows that he is the owner of these fields. This is the first time that we meet this fellow, and he is not nice to be around!

And he said to him, "Your brother has come, and your father has killed the fattened calf, because he has received him back safe and sound." But he became angry, and was not willing to go in. . .

The answer was succinct and said all that had happened in a sentence that is tight with excitement.

Your father has received your brother back safe and sound. The expression “safe and sound” on the surface simply means that he returned in health but much more than physical health. The word in the Hebrew language of the Old Testament is *shalom,* which means harmony, wholeness of person and with others; in this case it meant the son had returned to a harmonious, whole relationship and was reconciled with the father.

Shalom was used in greeting one another as those in covenant with the Lord meaning, “May you enjoy peace, harmony, and strength to your entire person in your walk with the Lord, and may our relationship and union be strengthened in Him.”

The few words of the village boy told the older son all he needed to know. The smell of food in the air and the sound of music and dancing was celebrating a restored union, reconciliation of father and son. He was hearing the uninhibited joy of a covenant meal binding in food and drink and rejoicing what had taken place on the road.

But he became angry. . .

By this time in the story it was obvious that the elder brother was the angry Pharisee, standing, watching the meal taking place between Jesus and the tax collectors. The parallel of the rising rage of the man at the idea of his young brother's acceptance and their own anger could not be lost on the hearers of the story.

This is the first time that we meet anger in the parable. The story has advanced in increasing waves of love—love that would not give up hope, that waited, and that had compassion and ran and kissed the returning son. In each of the parables in this chapter the owner of that which is lost is never depicted as angry or condemning but urgently going to seek out, find, and restore with great rejoicing the object of great worth. The older brother introduces a fury of moral anger directed at both the father and the son.

This man had no part in rejoicing with the father's joy. He could not comprehend what his father had done. In his world there was no place for love and forgiveness, only for keeping the rules and being rewarded or breaking them and being punished. His brother had clearly broken the rules, but so had the father by receiving him into a reconciled relationship without punishing him. His anger mounted as he strode toward the main house pushing his way through the joyous people.

. . . and was not willing to go in. . .

The custom of that day demanded that when a father entertained guests or gave a banquet in honor of someone, the eldest son took the position of host. The smooth running of the feast was in his hands, allowing the father to be free to visit with his guest of honor. The eldest son therefore did not sit at table but was at the door to greet and seat the guests, hovering making sure everyone was seated and served. Above all he made sure the honored guest was treated with the best the father's house could give. For the duration of the feast the eldest son became the head servant who served all. He was the face of the father and the family to all who were present. But in his rage at what he saw and had heard this son broke the custom and shamed his father before the village by refusing to even go in to the house. He refused to greet his brother and certainly would not serve him or anyone else at this feast of madness.

. . . and his father came out and began entreating him. . .

Refusing to go in and take his place as host and head servant was an insult to his father and to the guests. The watching villagers would be horrified at and ashamed for the father. It was expected that some punishment equal to such insulting behavior would be exacted immediately on the older son to save the face of the father. In such an important family the servants might have arrested him and held him until after the feast for the father's wrath. Instead the father personally and publicly left the table to go to where his fuming son insolently stood.

In the previous stories Jesus has told of the lost coin, the lost sheep, and the returning lost son, the one who finds has always taken the initiative and has gone out to where the lost is. Seeking love took the initiative by entering into the place of the lost one and laying hold to bring the lost object home to extreme rejoicing. The younger son had been met by urgent, seeking, running love to scoop him into its embrace. Jesus is making it plain that this moral upright son is as lost as his brother, and the father goes out to him even as he had so recently gone out to the younger son.

He does not go with fury to confront his unthinkable behavior with anger and threats but with love. The word Jesus used, *entreaty,* describes the father as coming alongside to encourage, even beseech, his son to come inside and take his rightful place. It is a word used of persuading and exhorting.

This son as he had come to the ranch to gain information had used the word *summoned,* a word meaning to call an inferior to stand in front of and answer a question. After the public insult he had delivered to his father that would be the word the listeners would expect Jesus to use when confronting the openly rebellious son. Instead he entreats him, not a face-to-face confrontation, but he comes alongside to persuade and encourage him to a change of mind. The word is used in 2 Corinthians 5:20! It is in the same family of words used to describe the Holy Spirit as the Comforter, convincing and drawing us to salvation. The father came to cool his son's anger and win him over.

But he answered and said to his father, "Look! For so many years I have been serving you, and I have never neglected a command of yours; and yet you have never given me a kid, that I might be merry with my friends. . ."

He had no time for his father's entreaty. His rage had been bottled up for years, and this was the tipping point where it boiled over, and nothing could contain it. In his anger he revealed how he perceived his identity in relation to his father with the words, *all these years have I served you.* The words as translated in our Bible would be bad enough, but the word is literally "I have been your slave." He did not see himself as the son and heir of the father but existing in abject slavery, repressed, and crushed under the control of a hard master. In society it was a demeaning scornful word describing a person who is neither a son nor even a friend. To use the word not only described his twisted view of his own identity but also that of his father. If he was a slave, then his father was a slave master, cruel and demanding, who had enslaved him. His work was a daily performance to gain his father's approval and avoid his disapproval. He lived under the burden of doing enough to earn the elusive reward that went with the approval. Such a life was a daily drudge, a boring performance without joy.

Now he compared his performance to that of his brother, and his world collapsed around him. In his world the brother should now be arrested and punished for the shame he had brought on the family while he should be honored with a feast celebrating his years of slaving on the ranch alone without the help of the brother. His father had disregarded all his performance; his life had been graded, and he had failed while his brother with no performance had gotten away with murder and sent to the top of the class. He felt that he was in the middle of a nightmare in which all the rules had been changed and the world was ruled by insanity.

This oldest son confused relationship with sacrifice; he "slaved" for his father, in effect saying, "See what I have given up for you while this other one was free enjoying his life!" Relationship may sacrifice, but sacrifice is not necessarily love. One may give all they have to the poor and even die as a martyr as a discipline without love (1 Corinthians 13:1f). When love sacrifices, it is with such joy that it is not recognized as suffering.

In his hurt rage, he revealed where his heart had been in all he had done for his father over the years. Every step he had taken was with resentment, envying those who were free of such bondage. He had been a bored slave, sucking it up, gritting his teeth, waiting for real life to begin when his efforts were recognized and rewarded. His miserable life is the perfect description of religion, practicing meaningless rituals, interpreting words, and believing that the worship of God is sacrificial disciplined boredom in the hope that one day it will be worth it when the rewards for life are handed out.

The resentment of years is spewed out in rage and disgust directed at his father. "No rewards, not even a paycheck for me! You have never thrown a party for me after all I have done, but this scoundrel comes crawling out of the gutter and you celebrate him! He gets the calf and I do not get even a goat! I have never been good enough for you; you obviously judge me as worthless."

He could not bring himself to call the returning son his brother but spat out the words *"this son of yours."* It was the announcement that he is no longer part of such an insane family. "If you call that scumbag your son, then count me out of this family and do not call me your son; treat me as the slave I am; honor and shower him with gifts and send me to the barn. I do not belong to such madness."

The structure, hopes, and expectancies that made up his life had crashed and burned in the moment he saw his brother accepted and honored. This was not a momentary reaction to the unexpected but the terrified rage of a man seeing his world collapse and all he had worked and lived for as being dismissed. His entire philosophy of life had been destroyed at the sight of his father's love for his brother. What he believed to be the meaning of life was so utterly other than that of his father that he would have to abandon his belief system and rebuild his life from the foundation up. He looked at unrelenting covenant love bestowed and received by faith in which performance had no part to play; all his efforts to do good and promises and works to avoid evil looked dead by comparison and fell apart as he beheld the joy of love. Life was not about performance but love, but the thought and sight of it sent him into blind rage.

19

My Dear Child

And he said to him, "My child. . ."

The father's words were gentle and reached past the furious words of his son. He addressed him as *my child.* The father disregarded everything the man has said about slavery, ignored his pointed self-exclusion from the family, and instead addressed him according to his true identity as his child.

And he said to him, "My child. . ." The words could be better translated as "my dear beloved son." In addressing both his sons the father consistently ignored their blind ignorance as to their true identity and addressed them only as he knew them to be. Both of the sons saw and spoke of themselves as excluded from the family and outside the circle of his love; both saw themselves as slaves of one kind or another. The father answered them both with strong words of their inclusion and how he saw them as his beloved children.

". . . you have always been with me. . ."

Throughout the years the father and this son had been living together on the same property, sitting face to face across the table, participating in the same family meal, discussing the business of their joint ownership of the ranch. It was beyond belief that this man identified with a slave.

". . . and all that is mine is yours. . ."

At the dividing of the inheritance when the younger son left home this son received his double portion. He was working on what was and would become his property when the father died. The father was saying, "This is your land, these are your animals—the abundance of this place is yours to enjoy! You can party every day of the week if you wish; it is yours to do as you will."

The father had given everything and reminded the son that *all that is mine is yours* held in joint ownership. Yet this son had believed in his heart that he was a slave and interpreted his life and relationship with his father through that mindset.

In his tortured mind everything the father had given and was already his must now be earned and deserved; what he owned he worked feverishly to receive one day as a reward. The father spoke in the present tense: all that *is* mine *is* yours, even while the son could only envision it as an elusive future reward assuming that he would do enough good to deserve it. He lived in the midst of abundance but did not enjoy it; mentally he lived in practical poverty.

Law is incapable of receiving a gift; we need grace to receive grace! Law coupled with the flesh is driven to earn, to deserve the blessings that only love can give. Sin involves trying to tear from God's hand what God-love wills to freely give. This son lived in the middle of gifts and blessing that were his inheritance, but he was blinded to it all in his obsession to deserve it, which festered as the frustration of never being good enough.

On the road earlier that day the younger son discovered that in capitulating to love, he received the inheritance that was infinitely more than the cash he called his inheritance at the beginning of the story.

He could not think of a love that originated solely in who the father was. He believed that his father's affection for him was based on his slavish obedience and his sacrificial work. In his twisted world his father must reject his brother as a failure to be punished and cast out in order to receive, acknowledge, and accept him. He is furious as he as an outsider looking into his father's world where he saw his younger brother accepted and celebrated.

His universe was turned upside down. In his world the boy must be punished; in the father's world there must be celebratory joy. His father's world was in such conflict with his that he had to declare that he was divorced from the father and no longer part of the family.

At this point in the story it was obvious that Jesus was speaking directly to the Pharisees and their mindset. They were blind to the loving heart of God and could not comprehend that within that love all of God's bounty was given. For them their performed goodness and avoidance of evil would buy them a place of distinction and favor with God. These religious men worked to keep the Law of God and added a multitude of their own making, hoping that their false god would be impressed. To suggest that true life and acceptance with God was found in trusting and receiving His love bordered on insanity! To think that there was love and favor to one who had not kept the rules, who had done evil and not good, but was now entrusted with accepting love was unthinkable. Their entire system of belief was rooted in acceptance or rejection according to performance. Their rage was out of fear that their foundational belief system was threatened and would collapse before what Jesus was saying.

The son could not enjoy his status in the father's house without his younger brother being punished for not keeping the rules he had set for himself. Comparison was part of their assurance of acceptance. Jesus had pointed this out in another story he told:

> And He also told this parable to certain ones who trusted in themselves that they were righteous, and viewed others with contempt: "Two men

> went up into the temple to pray, one a Pharisee, and the other a tax-gatherer. The Pharisee stood and was praying thus to himself, 'God, I thank Thee that I am not like other people: swindlers, unjust, adulterers, or even like this tax-gatherer. I fast twice a week; I pay tithes of all that I get.'" (Luke 18:9f)

The smug satisfaction gained by comparison with the behavior of others was the life support of their religious system.

In this story Jesus is describing God's justice that made whole the broken, mending and restoring all that had been lost to bring about reconciliation and relationship in his love.

Look at what is happening in terms of a court of law. The elder is bringing a suit against his father for the way he is treating the prodigal. The treatment, attitude, and favor the father shows to the boy is unthinkable. The elder presents his burden of proof in the list of his works: *"I have slaved. . . I have never. . ."* He is bringing the timesheet with all the hours worked and the unnoticed work around the ranch. His conclusion is that he is the perfect son; arrest the boy, bring him to judgment, and expel him from the family!

But the judge says that is baseless; a family is based on covenant love and trust—you speak of yourself as a slave that works for father and you are full of resentment against your brother. You have replaced the covenant with an unwritten contract within your own head and imagination never discussed with your father. Your father continues to act within covenant (all I have is yours) to which you have never responded. You lived in the spread feast of covenant but never received or implemented it but continued to be obsessed with the self-written contract.

The father's only counterclaim was to declare the covenant and his continuing love.

Pharisee justice was to punish the rule breakers and in so doing bring honor to the rule keepers. The hope of reward was reinforced by the assurance of punishment for all outside of their circle. They could not accept a heaven that did not have a hell full of those who had been stupid enough to ignore their moral teaching! Hell for others was a necessity to their enjoying heaven. In their eyes, Jesus sitting at table with tax collectors was his sitting in hell telling these rogues that they were favored and beloved of God and the door was open for them to leave.

Jesus captured their mindset in this elder son; his being loved and accepted had to include his brother's rejection and punishment; part of his heaven was the knowledge that his brother was in hell.

The elder brother's world was unravelling before his, collapsing at the sight of his father's love. Grace collapses the entire world built by law. In order to hold on to his religious sanity, he divorced himself from what he perceived as the insanity of his father's love. It is the religious that perceive they have everything to lose from accepting grace.

Jesus masterfully shows that the refusal of grace is exposed as the ultimate sin and rejection of the father. This son ended up in the chosen darkness made even darker in contrast by the radiant light of the party of love and grace. Although his love always extended to the Pharisees and religious leaders right through to the cross where he called for them to be forgiven, he makes it abundantly clear that what they proclaimed as truth was of Satan the liar and belonged to the company of the snake and viper—the place of the tombs of the dead.

The idea of the way of God not being the pursuit of good and rejection of evil is unthinkable; to entertain the thought that the dedication and discipline of keeping the letter of the Law was the satanic agenda from the beginning is horrifying to multitudes. But Jesus said exactly that; when addressing the Pharisees he described their doctrine as having been spawned of the devil:

> You are of your father the devil, and you want to do the desires of your father. He was a murderer from the beginning, and does not stand in the truth, because there is no truth in him. Whenever he speaks a lie, he speaks from his own nature; for he is a liar, and the father of lies. But because I speak the truth, you do not believe Me. (John 8:44–45)

The difference between the message of Jesus and that of the Pharisees was a chasm that could not be bridged; it was not that they needed Jesus to give a little adjustment to their message or to renovate an otherwise sound building. The only hope was in tearing down the building and beginning again with a new blueprint and a new foundation.

This was the worst moment of the elder son. He was defying his father, dishonoring and shaming him before the village, portraying him as a cruel mean slave master. He screamed in his father's face that he was not part of this family of love and forgiveness and wanted no part of the madness that was taking place. It was at that precise moment the father declared him to be his beloved son and joint owner of all that he has! It is at the revelation of the enormity of our hearts bent on sin that God's love and grace is revealed in fullness. Where sin abounds, grace abounds all the more!

"But we had to be merry and rejoice, for this brother of yours was dead and has begun to live, and was lost and has been found."

There is no ending to the story—we are its end in our alignment with one of the sons in relation to the speaker and main actor, Jesus.

20

Who Brought the Son Home?

The parable of the lost son is set in the context of two other parables, *the lost sheep* and *the lost coin.* Each of these stories has a seeker who counts the lost item so precious as to have their world turned upside down in order to do whatever it would take to find and restore the lost item. We must also understand that these parables are set in the context of the life of Jesus and His own definition of his mission of being sent to *seek and save* that which is lost.

The idea of seeking and saving the lost is rooted in the promises of the prophet Ezekiel in chapter 34 of his prophecy. In that chapter he exposes the false religious leaders and then announces

> "For thus says the Lord God, 'Behold I Myself will search for My sheep and seek them out. . .'" (Ezekiel 34:11)

Jesus was obviously referring to this passage, and it would not be missed by that first audience. In Luke 15 the Ezekiel passage is fleshed out and builds through the shepherd risking all to seek and find the sheep, the woman turning the house inside out in seeking and finding the lost coin, and it comes to its finale in the return of the lost son.

But the question is *who went to seek and to find the lost son?* The father announced to the servants and villagers that this was his son who had been lost but was now found but does not tell us who had gone to the far country to seek and find him. Of course there is no mystery searcher that has been lurking in the story unnoticed! But Jesus used the term and in the blatant meaning of the story to the listeners there was a seeker who successfully found the lost son.

In an ideal family bound by covenant the elder brother would go to seek out his brother and rescue him from starvation and attempt to bring about his restoration. In the family life of the Old Testament Israel it was spelled out. If a person or family found themselves in dire straits, starving and unable to pay their bills and forced to sell their inheritance, they were to appeal to a close relative for help. The close kinsman was called the *Goel,* which translates to our English word *redeemer.* It was a duty of covenant love that the *goel* would assume the debts and condition of their relative who in that society would not only lose their inheritance but in all probability be taken as a slave to pay off their debts. The *goel* would pay the debts and make their relative whole. They took the position of a savior.

In the story as Jesus told it there was no *goel*—the only candidate was the elder brother, and he would have happily seen his nearest kinsman perish in the far country and good riddance!

The story does not fit the other two. The sheep was lost and did not wake up one morning and decide to head for the sheepfold! It was in every way unable to find its way home. Likewise the coin had nothing to do with its finding but was returned to its rightful place by the initiative of the woman. But of the lost son Jesus simply said that he came to himself and followed the memory of a generous father and the joy of the recipients of his bounty. I have to ask again: *who went into the wilderness of the far country? Who went into the darkness and hopelessness of the young man's mind and was the word of hope of a father's love? Who went where he was to bring him home to where he belonged?* Are we no longer seeing the seeking God in this parable of the lost son?

Remember that the three parables were given to explain to His hearers why He was sitting as a friend in fellowship with the untouchable tax collectors and sinners. In the eyes of the religious watchers Jesus was sitting among those they deemed as abominable as pigs.

The story Jesus told is taking place right in front of their eyes! Jesus is telling the story from where He is sitting with the lost sons in their far country! Jesus is the ultimate Seeker, the true Elder Brother who has come into our far country to bring us home to the place in the Father's heart for which we were created.

Jesus is the Father's Son who from before time and space knew the Father's heart intimately; He was the delight of the Father and was the perfect image of the Father. He is the Creator of all that is and has now been sent by the Father into the sin-blasted world to take up residence inside the ghetto of our far country in the darkness and confusion of our fallen minds. He assumed our humanity and became fully and authentically Man joining us in our lost and sinful lives yet without sin. Hebrews 2:11 tells us that He became flesh and blood that He might call us his brothers and sisters. He became human that He might be our *Goel,* the close relative who assumes our debts and lost condition to restore all that we were created to enjoy. He is God sent from God to seek and save the lost.

He came into our far country, which is the arid desert of our dark thoughts of the Father arising from the lie of the accuser. We are so blind that we believe as final truth the voice of Satan accusing and condemning us, defining us as unworthy to hope for anything from God except the assurance of our inevitable rejection. Even worse we believe Satan's voice in our minds to be the voice of God and cower before him. Jesus tells us plainly that in the entire human race He alone knows the Father.

". . . no one knows the Son, except the Father; nor does anyone know the Father, except the Son, and anyone to whom the Son wills to reveal *Him*" (Matthew 11:27).

The word He used to describe his relationship with the Father, *know,* is not mere academic knowledge but intimate first-hand knowledge of the heart often used in Scripture to describe the marriage relationship. Jesus knows first-hand the love of the Father, and He has come into our terrible darkness to share with us His knowledge of the Father; that knowledge brings us out of our chosen darkness to our true home in friendship and relationship with God. He came from the light and glory of dwelling in the Father's love into the dark blindness of our hearts and minds and shed the light of the truth. He is the sound of joy and gladness that is in Father's house that calls us from the abyss of our hopelessness.

He has come inside our hearts and mind to tell us the final truth that we belong to the Family of the Father who loves us with passionate and unconditional love.

He has come where we are to take us to where He is in the heart of the Father.

The parable is taking place before the watching eyes of the hearers. The young lost man of the story came to himself. He heard the distant joy of love and generosity, and hope stirred within him that he dared to begin a journey back to where he belonged. Jesus is sitting with those designated as the pigs of society; His presence and words stir hope for these hopeless men who have believe that the accusing damning voices of religion and morality were the voice of God.

Jesus is the Father's Son sent to become our flesh and blood to be the sound of the true Father's music of compassion and longing for our return, the sound of hope that drew the lost boy home. He is the hope that informs the heart of the prodigal of a future beyond a pig herder's mind and imagination.

Jesus sitting at the table was only the preview of what was to happen in a few short months from that time. The sufferings and death of Jesus was a cosmic moment embracing all of time and all humans. He came to the very heart of where we sit in despair and death.

He took our sin, shame, and condition as described in 2 Corinthians 5 and Isaiah 53

> Surely our griefs He Himself bore,
> And our sorrows He carried;
> . . . But He was pierced through for our transgressions,
> He was crushed for our iniquities;
> The chastening for our well-being *fell* upon Him,
> And by His scourging we are healed.
> All of us like sheep have gone astray,
> Each of us has turned to his own way;
> But the LORD has caused the iniquity of us all
> To fall on Him. (Isaiah 53:4–6)

> . . . that one died for all, therefore all died; and He died for all, that they who live should no longer live for themselves, but for Him who died and rose again on their behalf. . . Therefore if any man is in Christ, *he is* a new creature; the old things passed away; behold, new things have come. Now all *these* things are from God, who reconciled us to Himself through Christ, and

> gave us the ministry of reconciliation, namely, that God was in Christ reconciling the world to Himself, not counting their trespasses against them, and He has committed to us the word of reconciliation. (2 Corinthians 5:14–19)

Our *Goel* has assumed our debt and broken relationship with the Father and in His resurrection leads us out to a new life of freedom from sin and the embrace of the Father who has never stopped loving us. It is significant that in describing that awakening of the young man sitting among the hogs Jesus had him say *"I will arise and go to my father."* The word *arise* is a specific word in the Greek used to describe resurrection from the dead—a strange word to describe getting up to go on a journey to the father. I believe that Jesus deliberately put that word in His parable anticipating His own resurrection when, in walking out of death and Satan's tyranny, He not only did it *for* us, but He carried us with him. He had made our history his history that His history might be our history; in *His* rising from the dead *we* are reborn into a new creation and relationship with the Father.

The words of the father to the returning son are also significant and would not be lost on the hearers. *This son of mine* echoes the word of the Father to His Son Jesus on more than one occasion.

> . . . and behold, a voice out of the heavens, saying, "This is My beloved Son, in whom I am well-pleased." (Matthew 3:17)

> . . . behold, a voice out of the cloud, saying, "This is My beloved Son, with whom I am well-pleased; listen to Him!" (Matthew 17:5)

Psalm 2 prophesied of Jesus in his resurrection and ascension with these words:

> I will surely tell of the decree of the LORD:
> He said to Me, "Thou art My Son,
> Today I have begotten Thee." (Psalm 2:7)

In one of the earliest sermons of Paul this verse of Psalm 2 is declared to be speaking of the resurrection of Jesus:

> And we preach to you the good news of the promise made to the fathers, that God has fulfilled this *promise* to our children in that He raised up Jesus, as it is also written in the second Psalm, "THOU ART MY SON; TODAY I HAVE BEGOTTEN THEE." (Acts 13:32–34)

This same Jesus comes into our fallen lives today; He speaks into our dark and broken minds and shares with us His knowledge of the Father. He assures us that we are the beloved of the Father loved even as the Father loves Him, and His arms of love are open to receive us with joy and celebration. He assures us that the tormenting voice we have heard is the voice of the accuser not the compassionate voice of the Father; we are not accused and condemned but beloved, forgiven, and accepted even as He is.

This is your true identity, hidden behind the walls and masks you may have erected. You are the one Jesus came to seek and save because of the infinite value the love of the triune God has placed upon you; He found you and joined you in your darkness and brought you home to the embrace of the Father in His resurrection and ascension. The Holy Spirit is the presence of Jesus now present with you to open your eyes so that you can arise and experience the embrace of the Father that has pursued you through all the days of your life.

> Father, I thank you for your unfailing and unconditional love for me that you revealed in Jesus. Thank you for showing me that I am of greater value to you than I have ever dreamed in my wildest imaginations. Tell me again and again in the depth of my soul of your love for me and the worth You place upon me.
>
> Open my eyes to see that in Jesus my past, present, and future are indissolubly bound up with You. Open my eyes that I might see myself as You see me.
>
> Holy Spirit, witness with my spirit that I am one with Jesus, and with Him belong to the Father forever. Be my strength and courage to walk around and manifest in my life the love You have to me.